RECORDED VERSIONS GUITAR

AUTHENTIC TRANSCRIPTIONS WITH NOTES AND TABLATURE

ACOUSTIC GUITAR 25TH ANNIVERSARY SONGBOOK

T0081337

ISBN 978-1-4950-1148-1

HAL•LEONARD® CORPORATION

7777 W. BLUEMOUND RD. P.O. BOX 13819 MILWAUKEE, WI 53213

Visit Hal Leonard Online at
www.halleonard.com

"Well, the Berlin Wall tumbled, Nelson Mandela walked free, McDonald's opened in Moscow, and MTV went acoustic"—that was the first sentence in one of the news stories from *Acoustic Guitar*'s inaugural issue in July 1990. A quarter-century later, the Berlin Wall is a distant memory; jailed revolutionary Mandela became president of South Africa, eventually dying of old age; and last year the Kremlin shuttered that McDonald's in Pushkin Square. But *MTV Unplugged* still airs occasionally, recently featuring (believe it or not) a rapping, twerking, Dolly Parton-covering Miley Cyrus backed by acoustic guitar, banjo, standup bass, upright piano, and drums.

And *AG* still publishes.

Such is the power of the acoustic guitar's sway on multiple generations of musicians. For the past 25 years, in hundreds of feature profiles, songs, gear reviews, and lessons, *AG* has assisted those musicians in learning or improving their technique, and in choosing the right instruments and gear for particular sounds and styles. The mission has been to introduce readers to the magic of the acoustic guitar in all its forms, especially through song.

But what is an "acoustic" song"? Is it a song played entirely on an acoustic guitar? Or is it a sound, a feel, a mindset?

It's all of these.

And within the *Acoustic Guitar Songbook* you'll find everything from haunting, pure acoustic blues to folk- and rock-based songs and everything in between.

The acoustic-guitar songbook is an ever-changing soundscape. The important thing is to play along … and to have fun!

Acoustic Guitar

Words and Music by Stephin Merritt

Tuning (low to high):
E-A-D-G-B-D

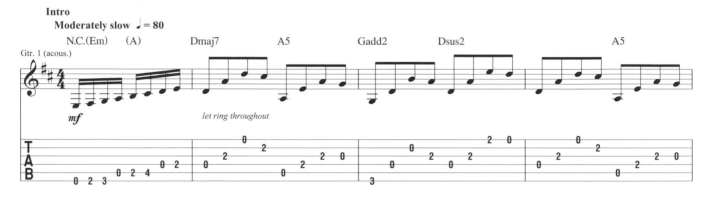

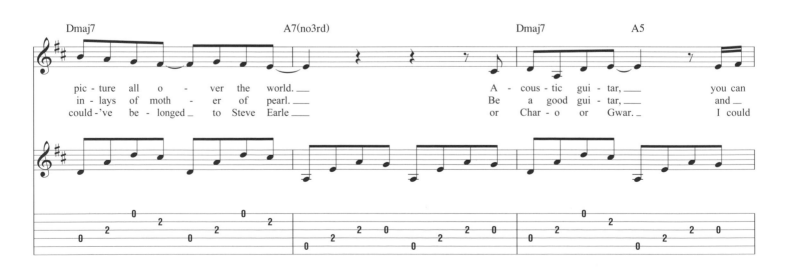

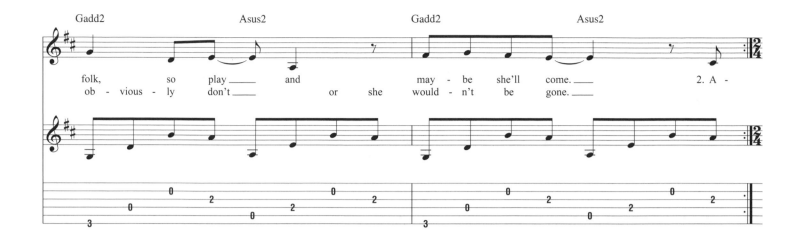

folk,   so   play ___   and   may - be   she'll   come. ___   2. A -
ob - vious - ly   don't ___   or   she   would - n't   be   gone. ___

Interlude

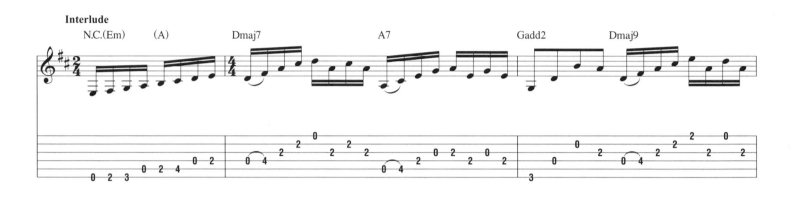

D.S. al Coda

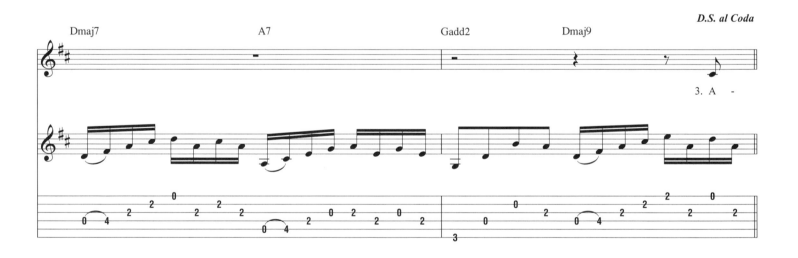

3. A -

⊕ **Coda**

girl. ___   You'd bet - ter   bring me   back ___   my   girl. ___

Pitch: B D G B   D G F♯

Angry Anymore

Words and Music by Ani DiFranco

Gtr. 2: tuning, capo III:
(low to high) E-B-B-F#-B-E

*Banjo arr. for gtr.

**Chord symbols reflect implied harmony.

***Symbols in parentheses represent chord names respective to capoed guitar.
Symbols above reflect actual sounding chords. Capoed fret is "0" in tab.

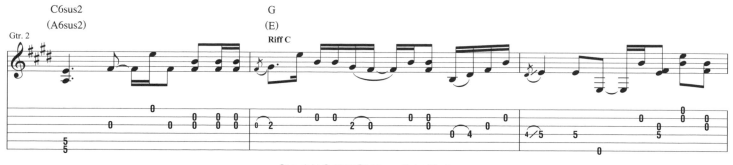

Interlude

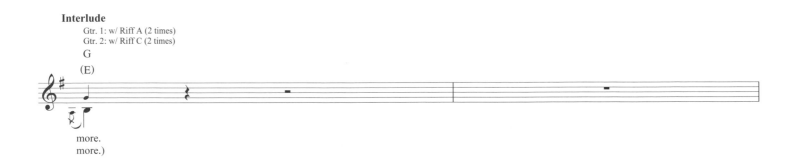

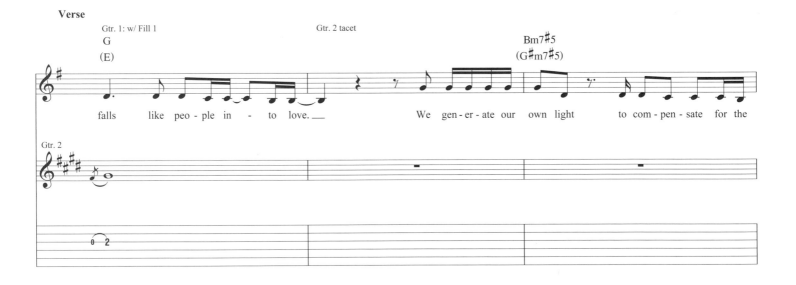

Verse

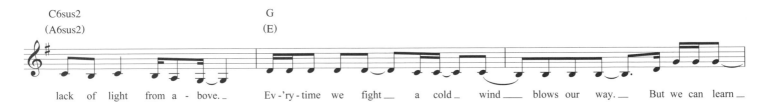

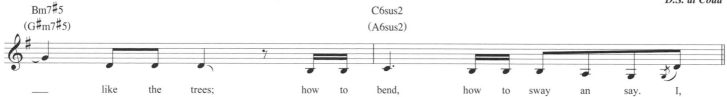

like the trees; how to bend, how to sway an say. I,

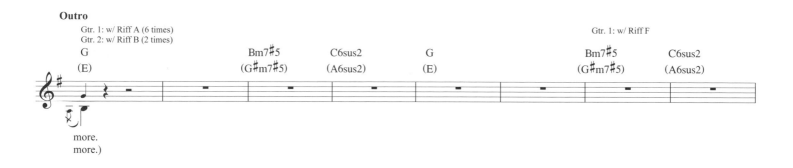

⊕ Coda

I'm _____
(I'm _____)

not an - gry an - y -
not an - gry an - y -

Outro

Gtr. 1: w/ Riff A (6 times)
Gtr. 2: w/ Riff B (2 times)

Gtr. 1: w/ Riff F

more.
more.)

from The Avett Brothers - *Emotionalism*

The Ballad of Love and Hate

Words and Music by Scott Avett, Seth Avett and Robert Crawford

Capo III

*Symbols in parentheses represent chord names respective to capoed guitar.
Symbols above reflect actual sounding chords. Capoed fret is "0" in tab.
Chord symbols reflect implied harmony.

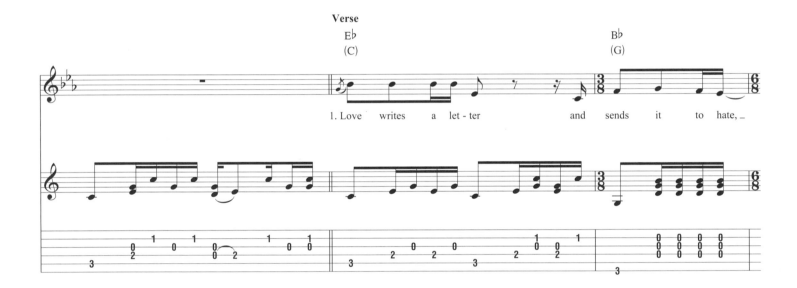

1. Love writes a let-ter and sends it to hate, _

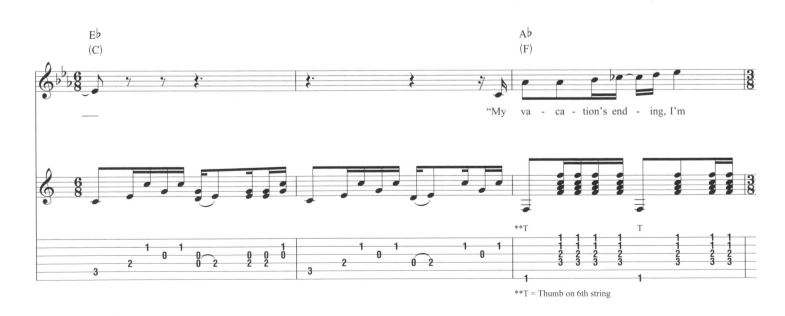

"My va-ca-tion's end-ing, I'm

**T = Thumb on 6th string

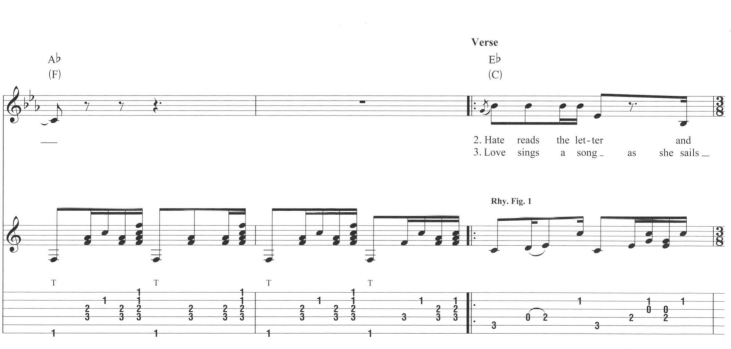

throws it a - way. _____
_____ through the sky.   "A,
                                                                                                        The

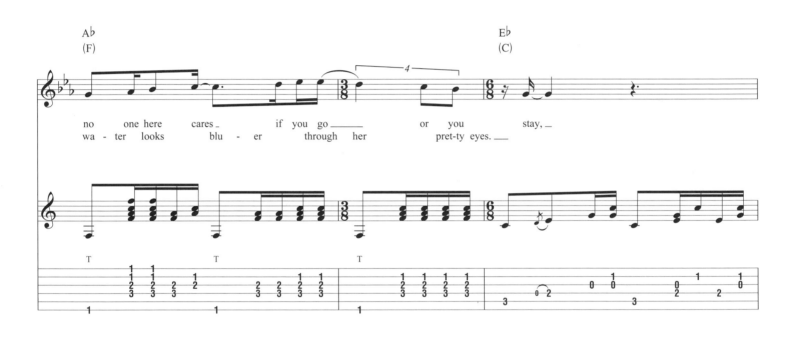

no one here cares ___ if you go _____ or you stay, ___
wa - ter looks blu - er through her pret-ty eyes. ___

I   bare - ly   e - ven   no - ticed   that   you   were   a - way, ___   I'll
And ev - 'ry-one knows ___ it   when - ev - er she flies _____ and

see you or I won't .... what - ev - er."
al - so .... when she comes down. _

End Rhy. Fig. 1

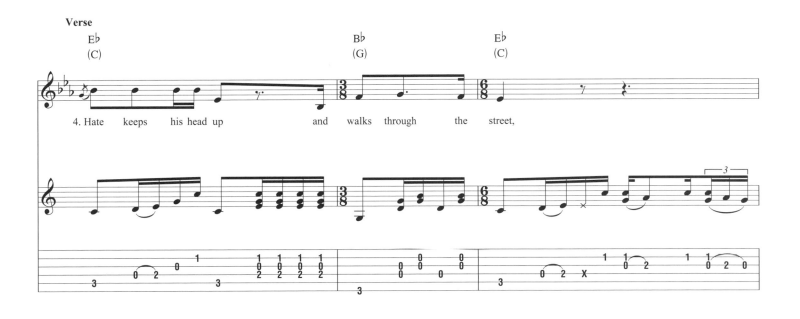

Verse

4. Hate keeps his head up .... and walks through the street,

ev - er - y stran - ger and .... drift - er he

greets, and shakes hands with ev - er - y

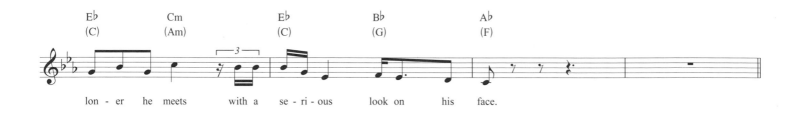

lon - er he meets with a se - ri - ous look on his face.

Verse

Gtr. 1: w/ Rhy. Fig. 1

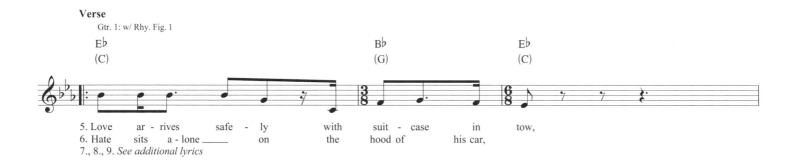

5. Love ar - rives safe - ly with suit - case in tow,
6. Hate sits a - lone on the hood of his car,
7., 8., 9. *See additional lyrics*

car - ry - ing with her the good things we know,
with - out much re - gard to the moon or the

stars, a rea - son to live and a
la - zi - ly kil - ling the

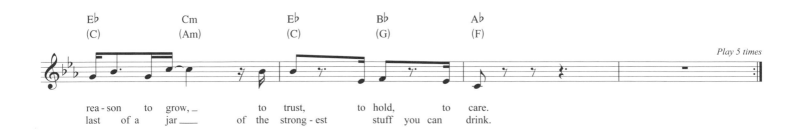

Play 5 times

rea - son to grow, to trust, to hold, to care.
last of a jar of the strong - est stuff you can drink.

Verse

10. Hate stum-bles for-ward and leans in the door, _____ wear - y head hung _ down, eyes _____ to the floor.

He says, "Love, I'm sor-ry," and she said, "What for? I'm yours _ _____ and that's it, what - ev - er." "I

should not have been _ gone _ for so _ long, _ I'm yours _ and that's it, for-

ev - er, you're mine and that's it, for - ev - er."

Additional Lyrics

7. Love takes a taxi, a young man drives
   As soon as he sees her, hope fills his eyes.
   But tears follow after, at the end of the ride,
   'Cause he might never see her again.

8. Hate gets home lucky to still be alive.
   He screams over the sidewalk and into the drive.
   The clock in the kitchen says two fifty-five,
   And the clock in the kitchen is slow.

9. Love has been waiting, patient and kind,
   Just wanting a phone call or some kind of sign,
   That the one that she cares for, who's out of his mind,
   Will make it back safe to her arms.

from The Beatles - (White Album)

Blackbird

Words and Music by John Lennon and Paul McCartney

Intro
Moderately slow ♩ = 93

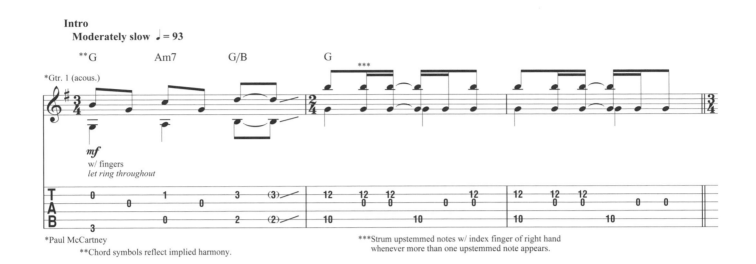

*Gtr. 1 (acous.)
mf
w/ fingers
let ring throughout

*Paul McCartney
**Chord symbols reflect implied harmony.

***Strum upstemmed notes w/ index finger of right hand
whenever more than one upstemmed note appears.

Verse

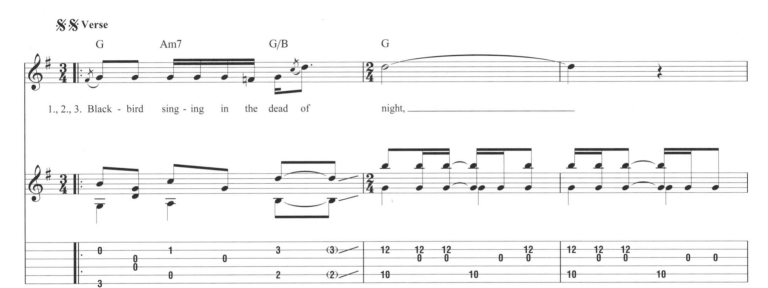

1., 2., 3. Black - bird sing - ing in the dead of night, _____

(1., 3.) take these bro - ken wings ____ and learn ____ to fly. ____
(2.) take these sunk - en eyes ____ and learn ____ to see. ____

in - to the light ___ of the dark black ___ night. ___

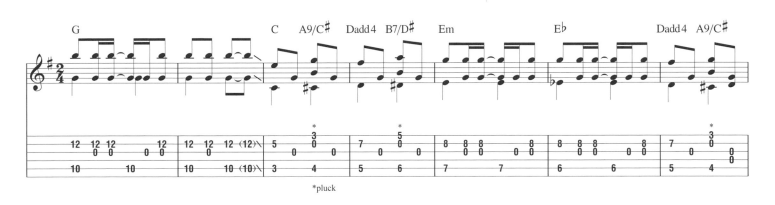

*pluck

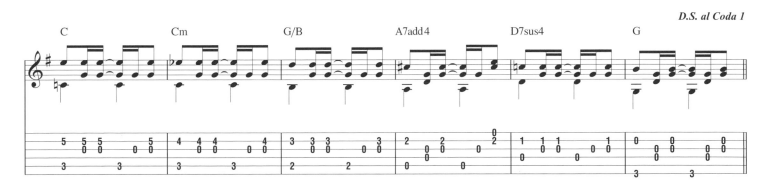

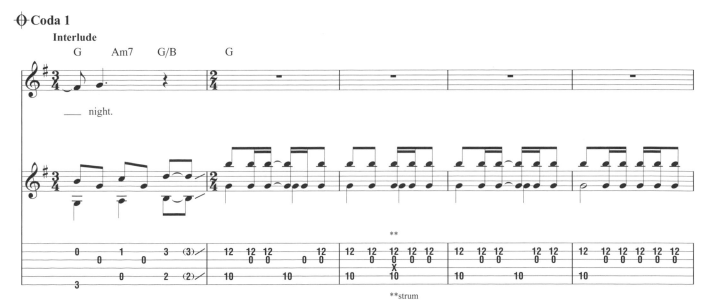

___ night.

**strum

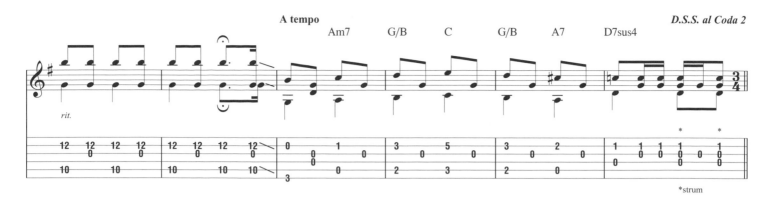

*strum

Coda 2

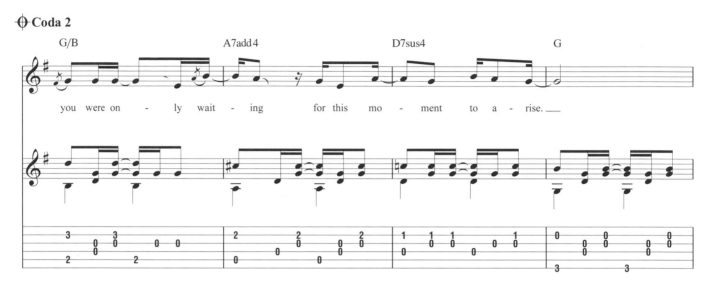

you were on - ly wait - ing   for this   mo - ment   to a - rise. __

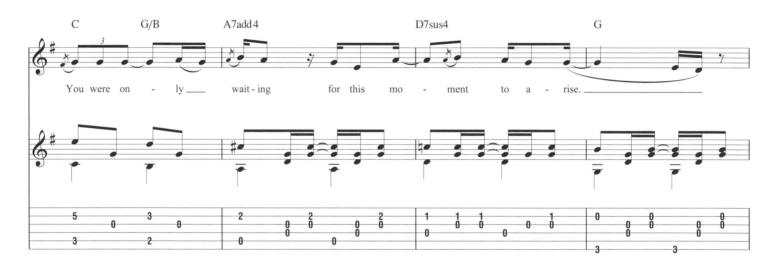

You were on - ly __   wait - ing   for this   mo - ment   to a - rise. _____

You were on - ly wait - ing ____   for this   mo - ment   to a - rise. ____

**Pat strings with fingers
of right hand.

Bron-Yr-Aur

Music by Jimmy Page

Open C6 tuning:
(low to high) C-A-C-G-C-E

Moderately slow ♩ = 86

*Chord symbols reflect implied harmony.
**Fade in

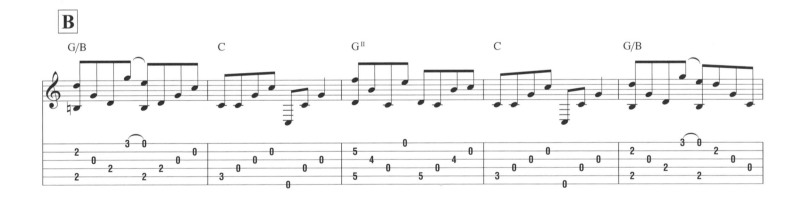

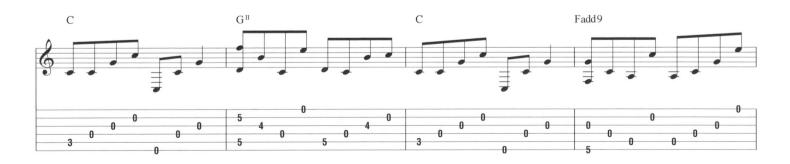

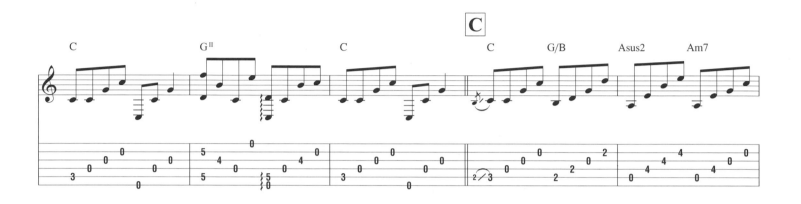

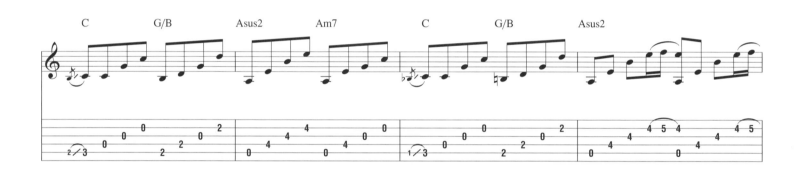

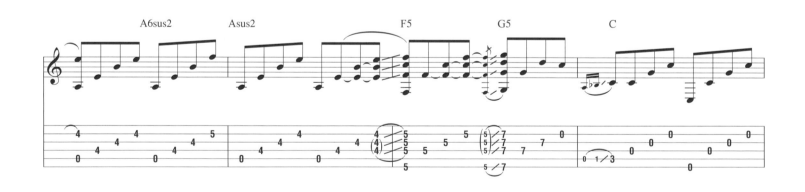

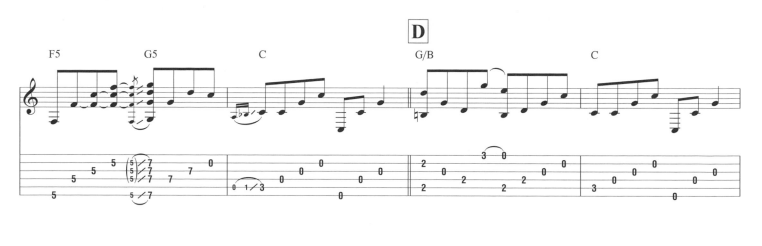

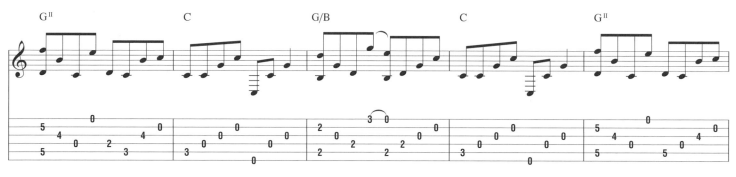

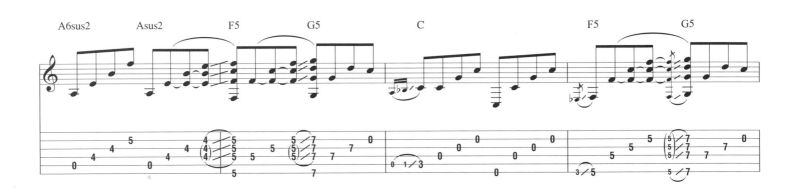

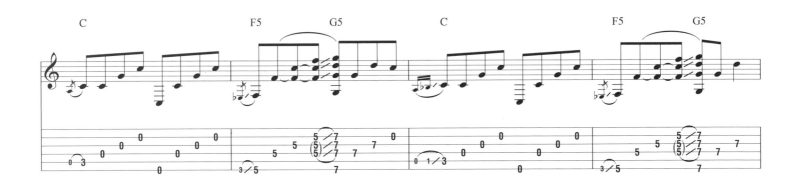

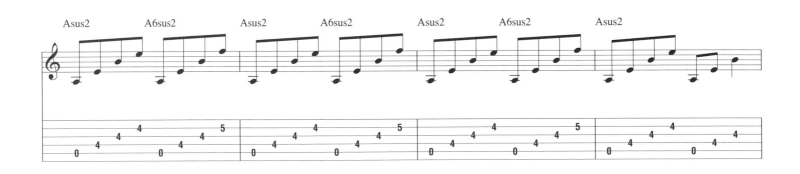

Corrina

Traditional

*Tune down approx. 1 1/2 steps:
(low to high) C#-F#-B-E-G#-C#

Intro
Moderately slow ♩ = 86

*Recording sounds approx. 1/4 step flat.

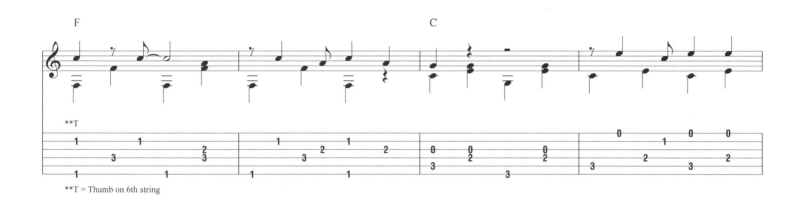

**T = Thumb on 6th string

1. Cor - ri - na, Cor -
2. I left Cor -

from Woody Guthrie - *The Asch Recordings*

Do Re Mi

Words and Music by Woody Guthrie

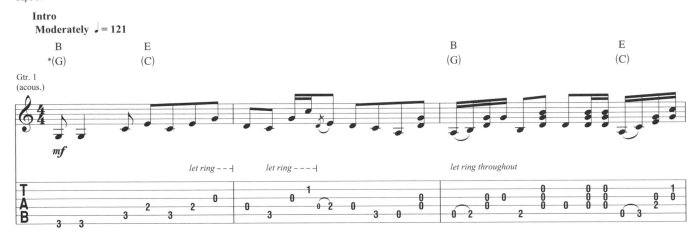

*Symbols in parentheses represent chord names respective to capoed guitar.
Symbols above reflect actual sounding chords. Capoed fret is "0" in tab.
Chord symbols reflect implied harmony.

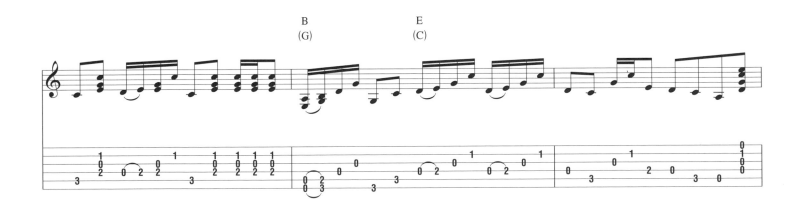

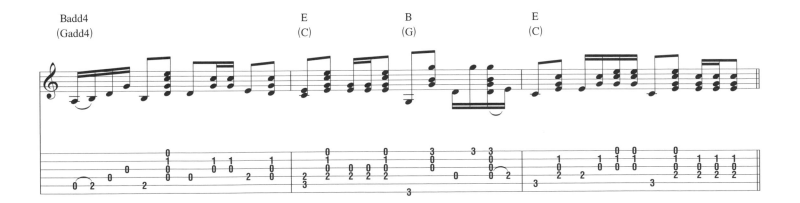

Verse

1. Lots of folks _ back East, they say, is leav - in' home ev - 'ry day,

beat - in' the hot old dust - y way _ to the Cal - i - for - nia line. _

End Rhy. Fig. 1

'Cross the des - ert sands they roll, get - tin' out _____ of that old _ dust bowl, they

think they're go-in' to a sug-ar bowl,__ but here's what they find.

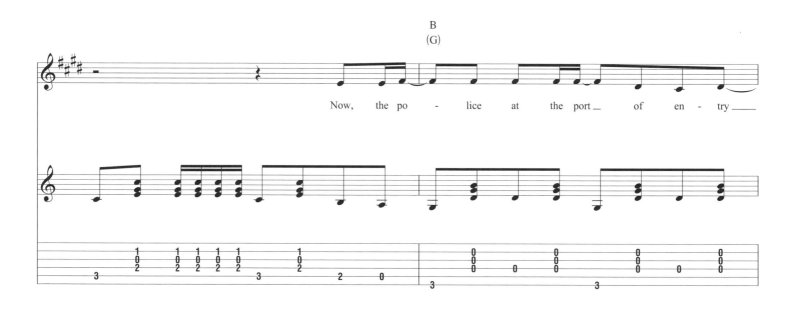

Now, the po - lice at the port__ of en - try __

__ say, "You're num - ber four - teen thou - sand for to -

E
(C)

day." Oh, if you ain't got the do re mi, { folks, } { boys, }

B
(G)

you ain't got the do re mi, why, you

bet-ter go back to beau-ti - ful Tex - as, O - kla-ho-

-ma, Kan-sas, Geor-gia, Ten-nes-see. ___ Cal - i -

for - nia is a gar - den of E - den, a

par - a - dise ___ to live in ___ or see, but be -

Verse
Gtr. 1: w/ Rhy. Fig. 1

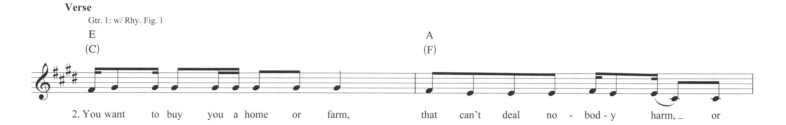

2. You want to buy you a home or farm, that can't deal no-bod-y harm, or

take your va-ca-tion by the moun-tains ___ or sea.

Don't swap your old cow ___ for a car, you bet-ter stay ___ right where you are, ___ you

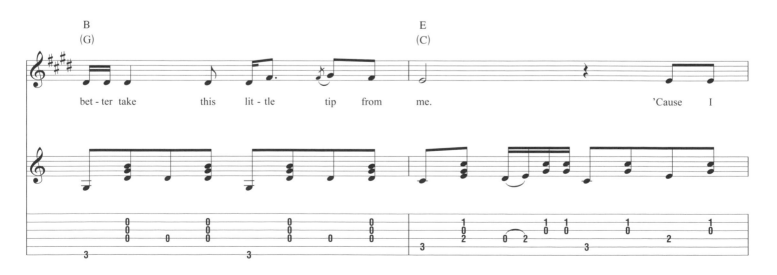

bet-ter take this lit-tle tip from me. 'Cause I

from Bob Dylan - *The Freewheelin' Bob Dylan*

Don't Think Twice, It's All Right

Words and Music by Bob Dylan

Capo IV

Intro
Moderately ♩ = 108

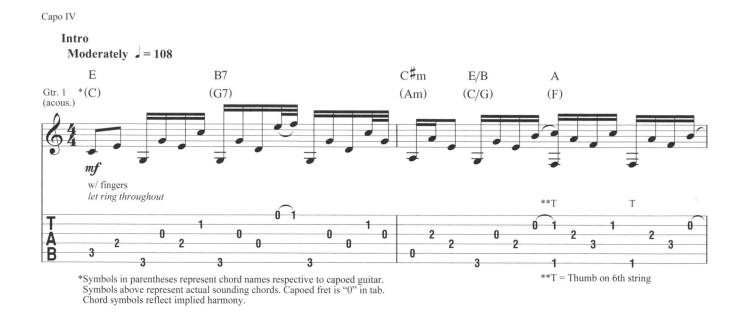

*Symbols in parentheses represent chord names respective to capoed guitar.
Symbols above represent actual sounding chords. Capoed fret is "0" in tab.
Chord symbols reflect implied harmony.

**T = Thumb on 6th string

1. Well, it ain't

Verse

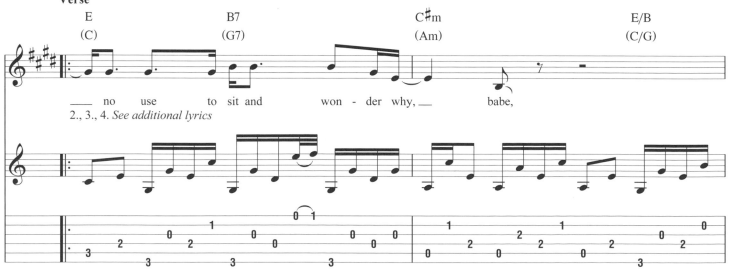

___ no use to sit and won-der why, ___ babe,

2., 3., 4. See additional lyrics

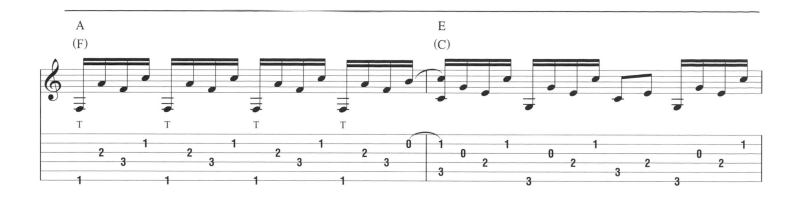

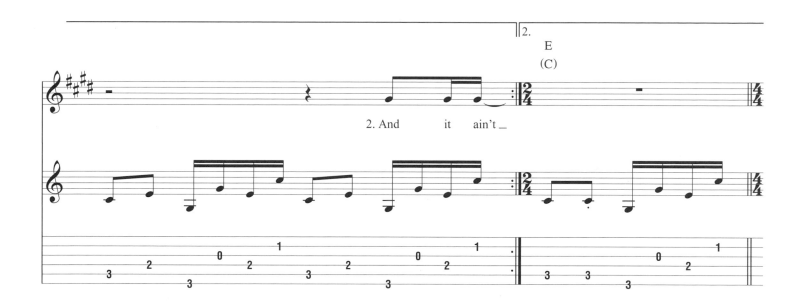

2. And it ain't

Interlude

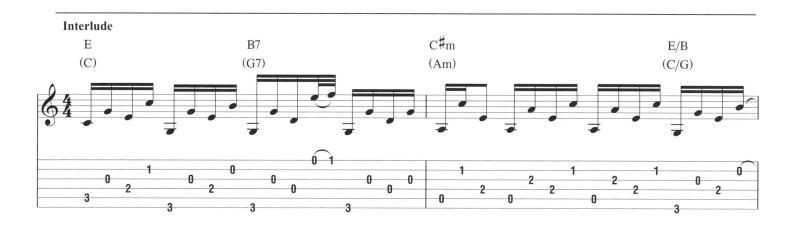

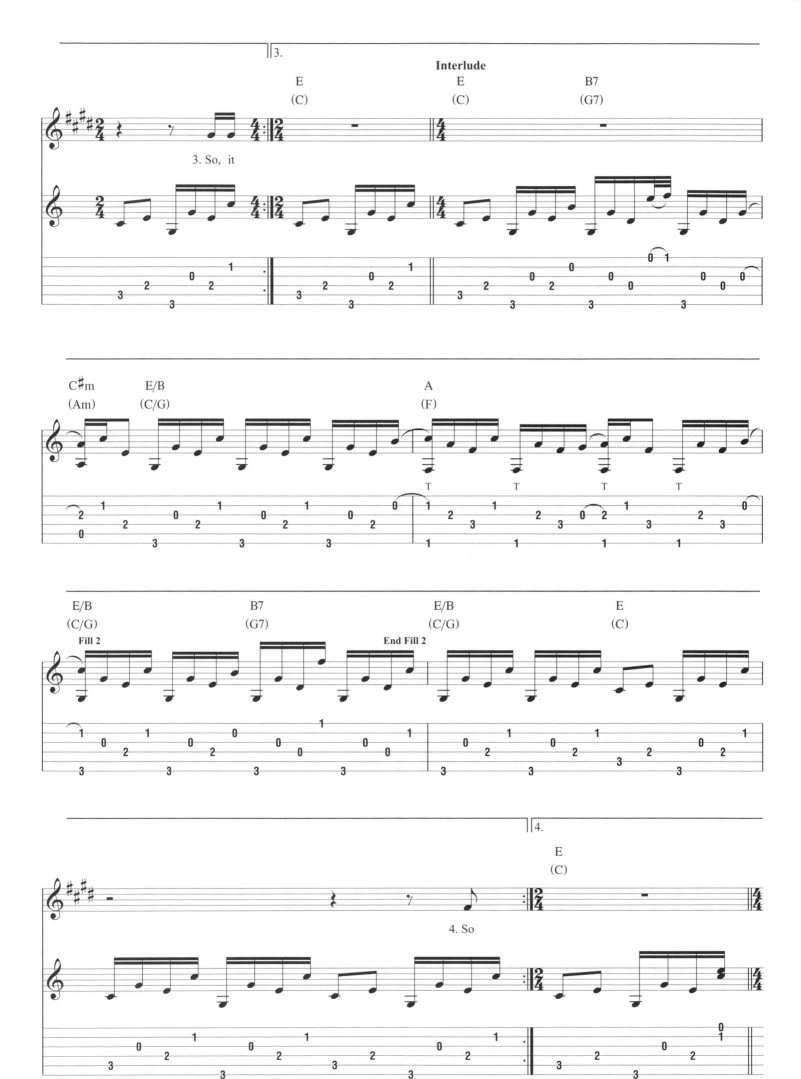

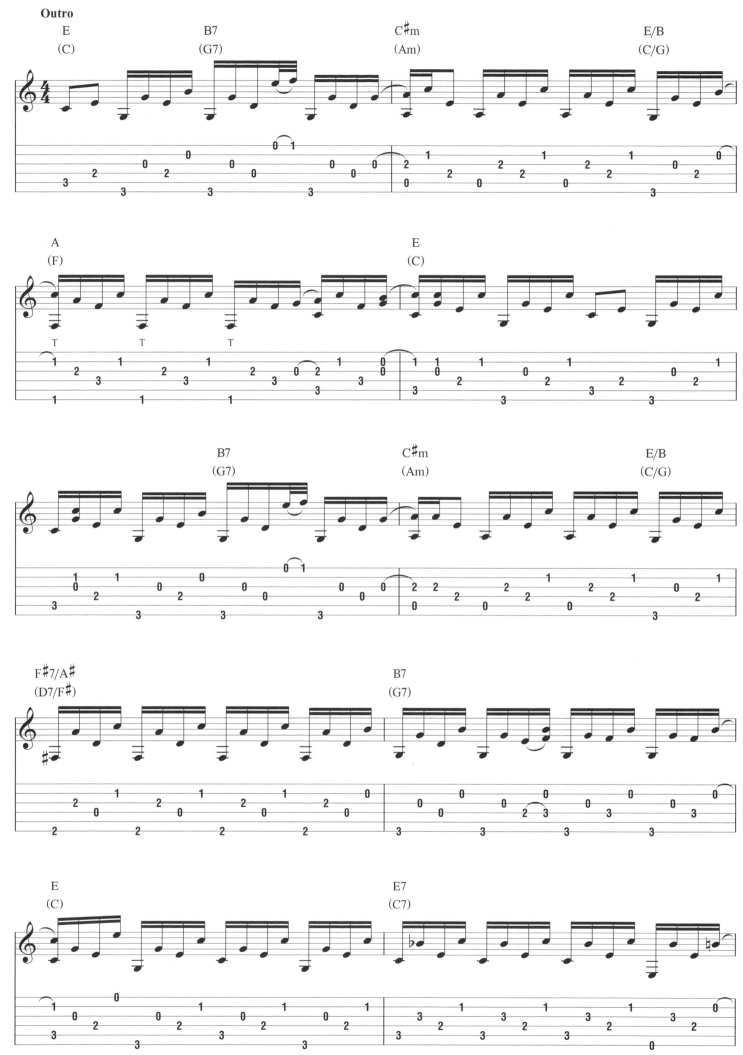

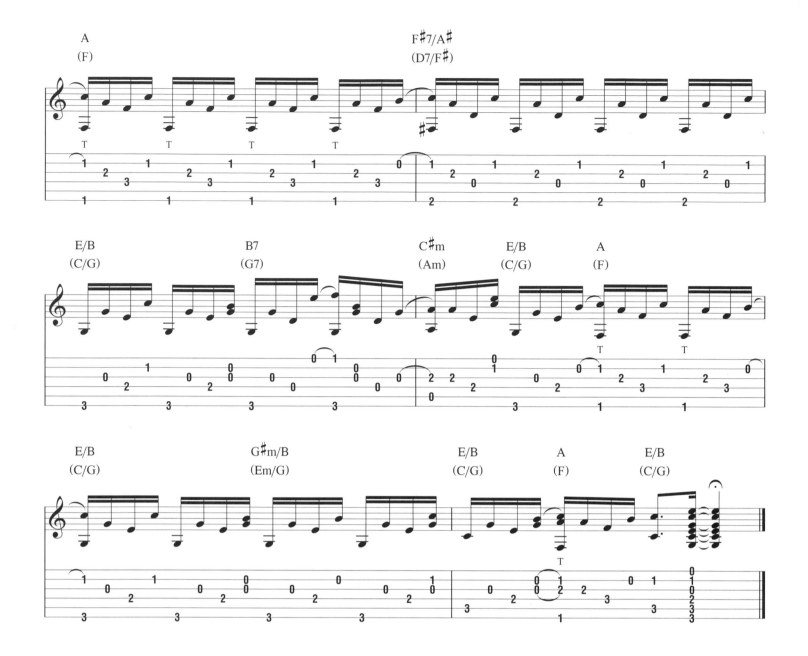

Additional Lyrics

2. And it ain't no use in turnin' on your light, babe,
   The light I never knowed.
   And it ain't no use in turnin' on your light, babe.
   I'm on the dark side of the road.
   But I wish there was somethin' you would do or say
   To try and make me change my mind and stay.
   But we never did too much talkin' anyway,
   But don't think twice, it's all right.

3. So it ain't no use in callin' out my name, gal,
   Like you never done before.
   And it ain't no use in callin' out my name, gal.
   I can't hear you anymore.
   I'm a, thinkin' and a, wonderin', walkin' down the road.
   I once loved a woman, a child I am told.
   I give her my heart, but she wanted my soul,
   But don't think twice, it's all right.

4. So long, honey, babe.
   Where I'm bound, I can't tell.
   Goodbye's too good a word, babe,
   So I'll just say fare thee well.
   I ain't sayin' you treated me unkind.
   You coulda done better, but I don't mind.
   You just kinda wasted my precious time,
   But don't think twice, it's all right.

from Elizabeth Cotten - *Freight Train and Other North Carolina Folk Songs*

Freight Train

Words and Music by Elizabeth Cotten

Tune down 1 step:
(low to high) D-G-C-F-A-D

Intro
Moderately slow ♩ = 95

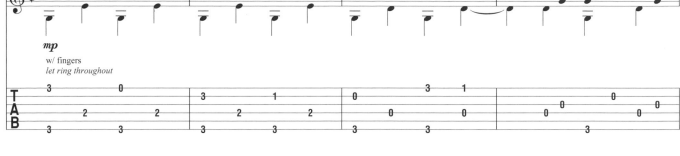

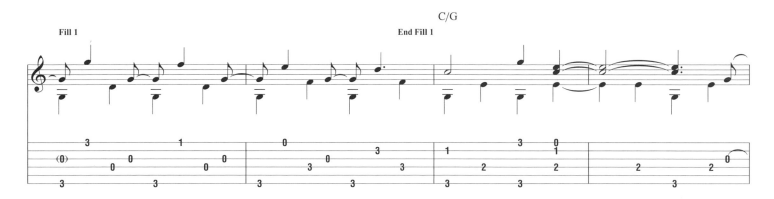

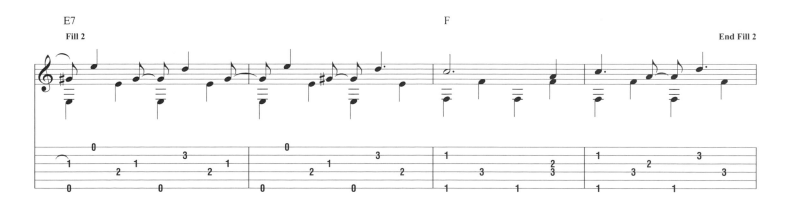

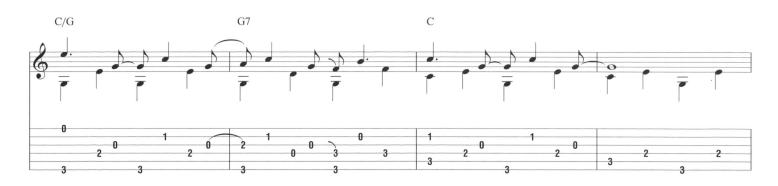

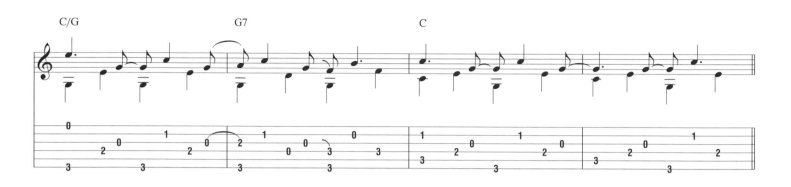

Verse

1. Freight train, freight train run so fast. _____
2. When I _____ am dead and _____ in my grave, _____
3. When I _____ die, _____ Lord, _____ bur - y me deep _____
4. *See additional lyrics*

2nd, 3rd & 4th times, Gtr. 1: w/ Fill 1

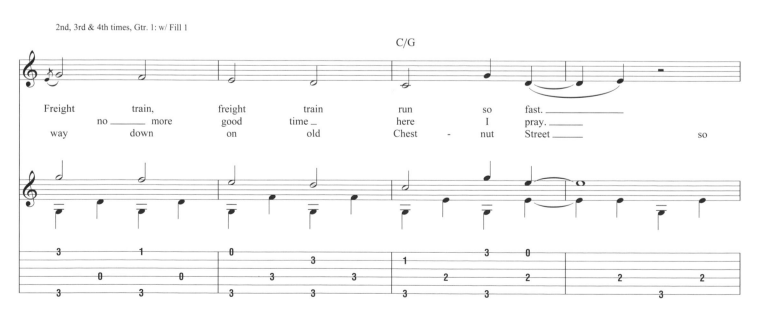

Freight train, freight train run so fast. _____
no _____ more good time _ here I pray. _____
way down on old Chest - nut Street _____ so

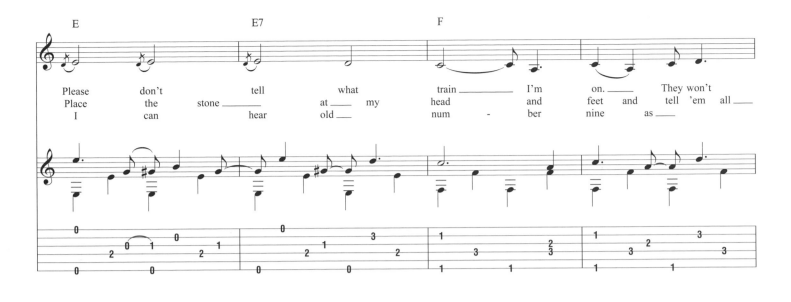

Please don't tell what train I'm on. They won't
Place the stone at my head and feet and tell 'em all
I can hear old num - ber nine as

know what route I've gone.
that I'm gone to sleep.
she came roll - in' by.

Interlude
2nd, 3rd & 4th times, Gtr. 1: w/ Fill 2

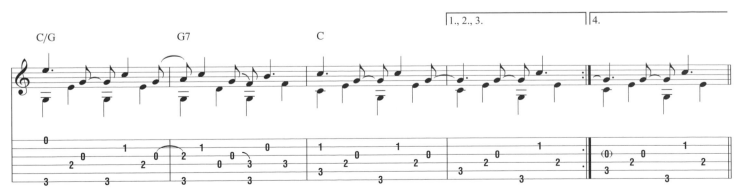

47

Additional Lyrics

4. When I die, Lord, bury me deep
   Way down on old Chestnut Street.
   Place the stone at my head and feet
   And tell 'em all that I'm gone to sleep.

from the *O Brother, Where Art Thou? Soundtrack* - Chris Thomas King

Hard Time Killing Floor Blues

Words and Music by Nehemiah "Skip" James

Open Dm tuning:
(low to high) D-A-D-F-A-D

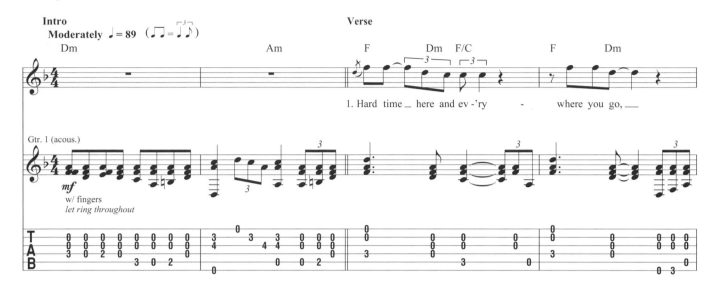

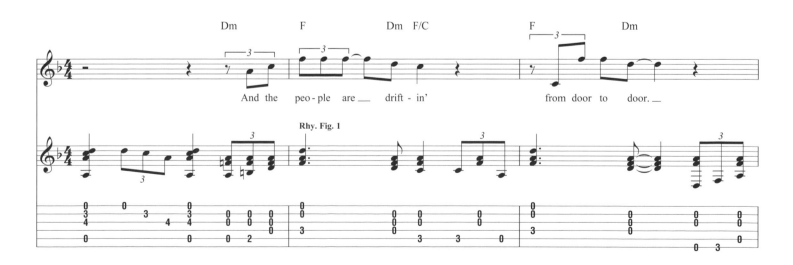

Hickory Wind

Words and Music by Gram Parsons and Bob Buchanan

Capo II

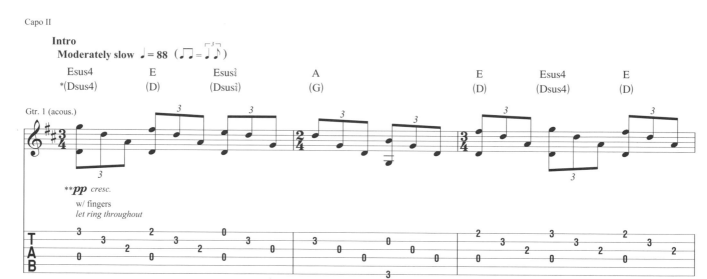

*Symbols in parentheses represent chord names respective to capoed guitar.
Symbols above reflect actual sounding chords. Capoed fret is "0" in tab.
Chord symbols reflect implied harmony.

**Fade in, next 5 meas.

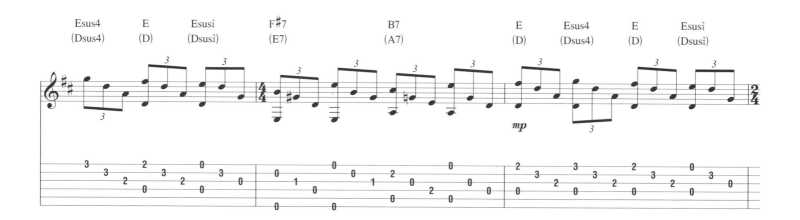

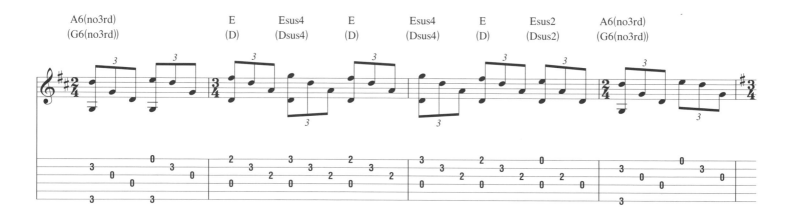

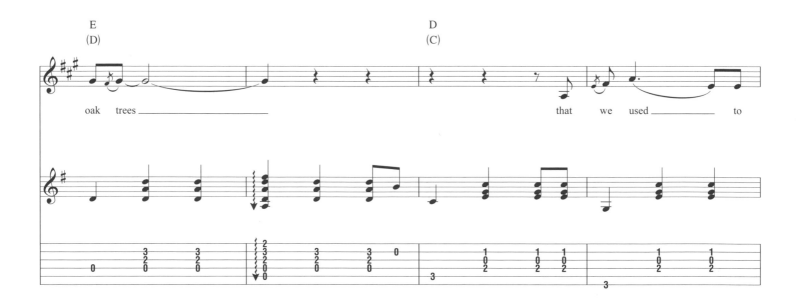

oak trees _____ that we used _____ to

climb. _____ But now when I'm

*Harmony vocal is female and sounds
one octave lower than written.

_____ lone - some, _____ I al - ways _____ pre -

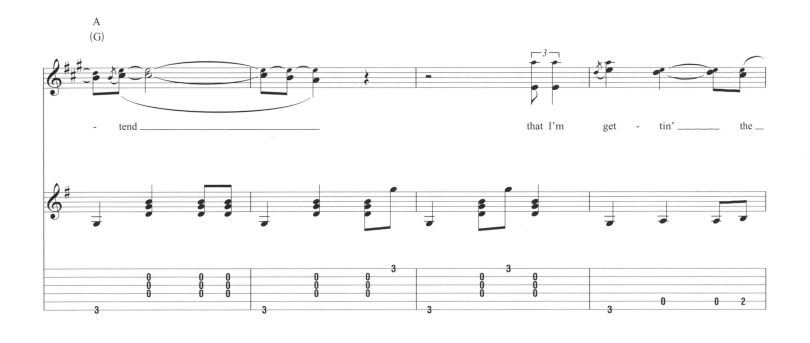

-tend _____ that I'm get - tin' _____ the _

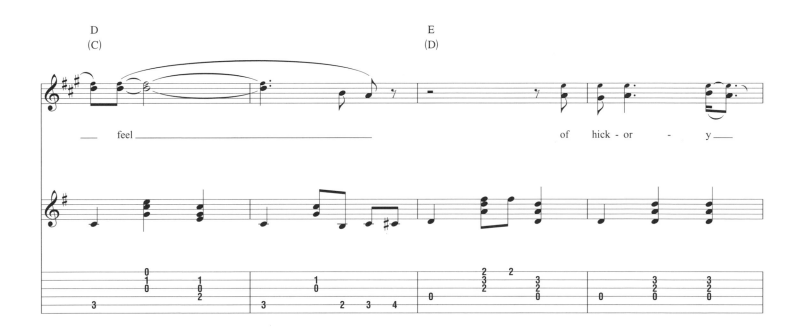

_ feel _____ of hick - or - y _____

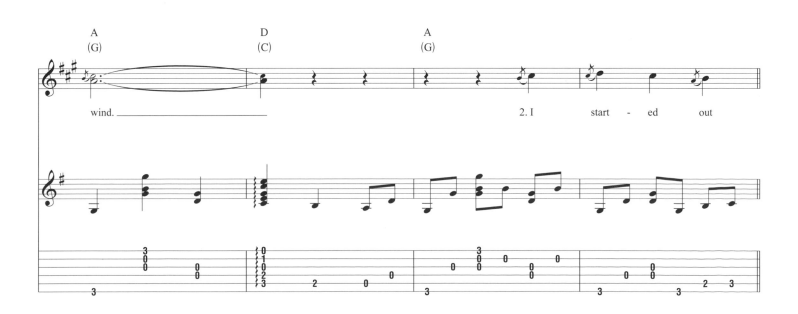

wind. _____ 2. I start - ed out

𝄌 Verse

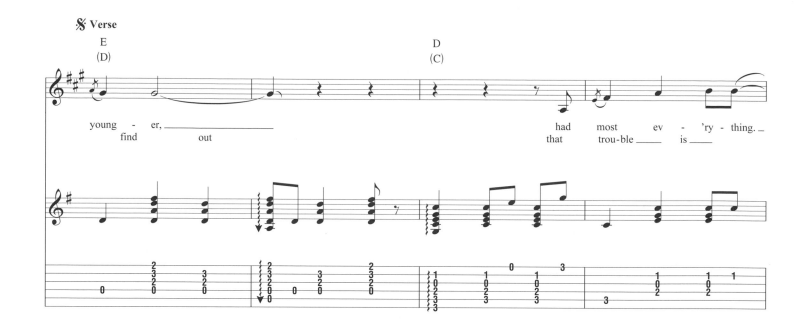

young - er, _____
find _____ out

had most ev - 'ry - thing. ___
that trou - ble _____ is _____

_____ real, _____
_____ in a far a - way _____

All the rich - es _____ and _____

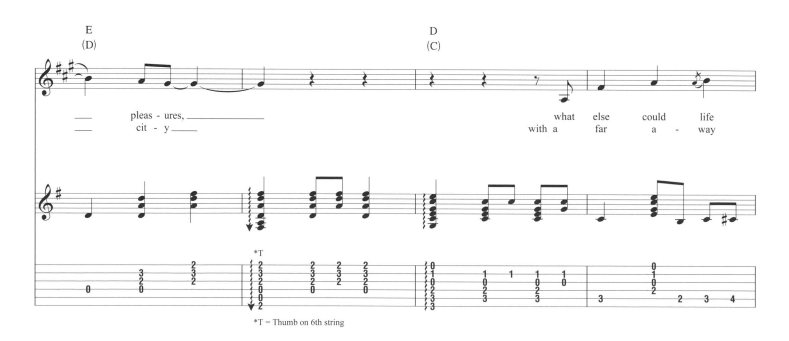

_____ pleas - ures, _____
_____ cit - y _____

what else could life
with a far a - way

*T = Thumb on 6th string

56

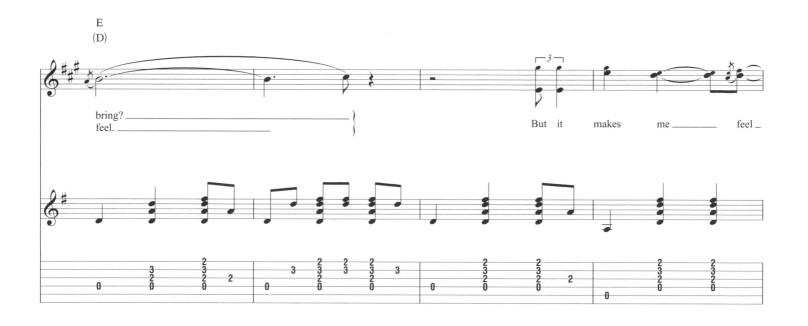

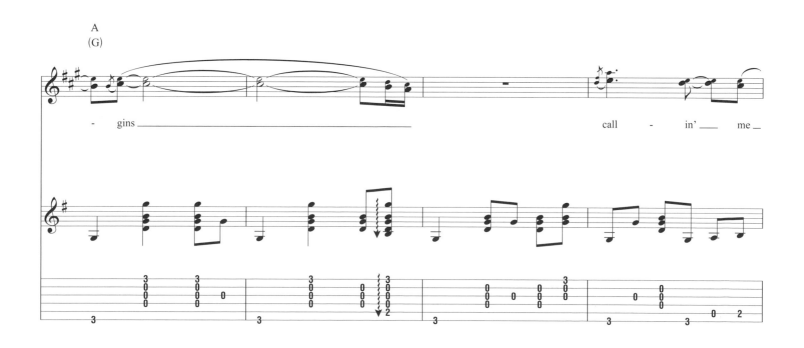

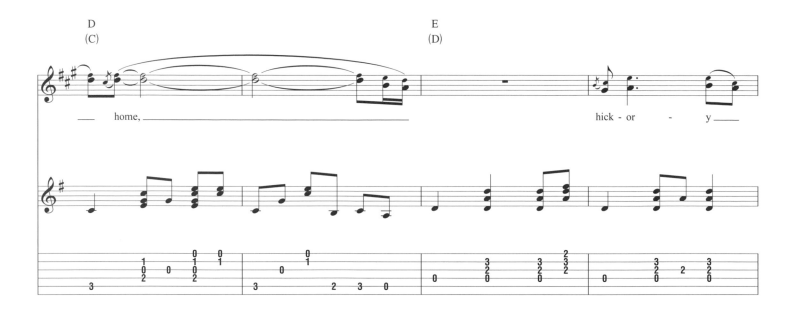

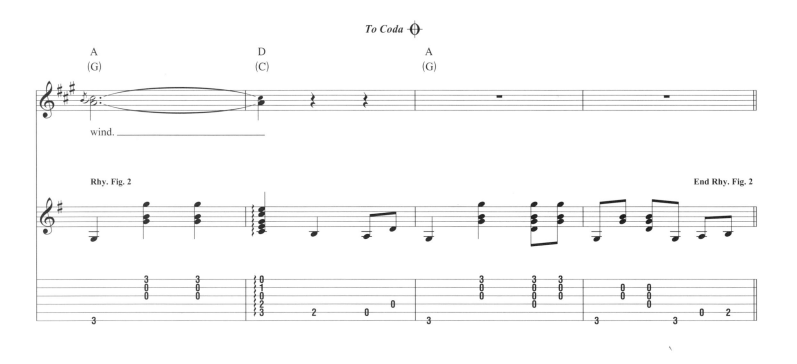

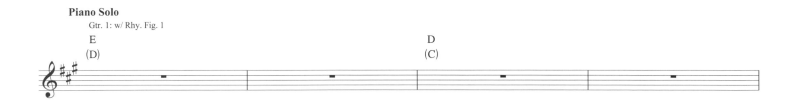

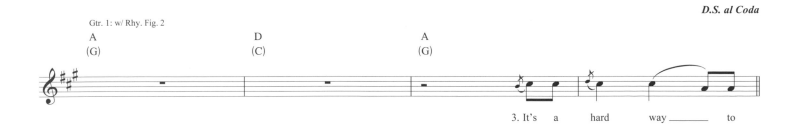

⊕ Coda

Keeps call - ing ___ me ___ home, ___

hick - or - y ___

wind. ___

Hope of a Lifetime

Words and Music by Kenneth Pattengale and Joseph Ryan

Gtr. 1: Capo VIII
Gtr. 2: Tune down 1 step, capo V:
(low to high) D-G-C-F-A-D

*Symbols in single parentheses represent chord names respective to capoed Gtr. 1. Symbols in double parentheses represent chord names respective to capoed Gtr. 2. Symbols above reflect actual sounding chords. Capoed fret is "0" in tab. Chord symbols reflect implied harmony.

**2nd string bumped with pull-off finger.

calm   wind   in   the   pine,   for   the

fate   of   a   fear - some   trav - es - ty

seems to have for - got - ten me, __

seems to have for - got - ten me. _____ If it

End Rhy. Fig. 2

by the stars, on their own,

by the stars, on their own. 2. While I

End Rhy. Fig. 3

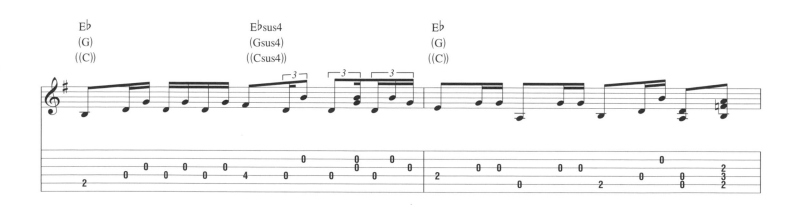

70

Verse

Gtr. 2: w/ Rhy. Fig. 2

new - found rev - er - ie

Gtr. 1

qui - et peace I found,

by the stars, _____ on their own. _____

Outro

Gtr. 2: w/ Rhy. Fig. 1 (1st 4 meas.)

In the Pines (Black Girl)

New Words and New Music Adaptation by Huddie Ledbetter

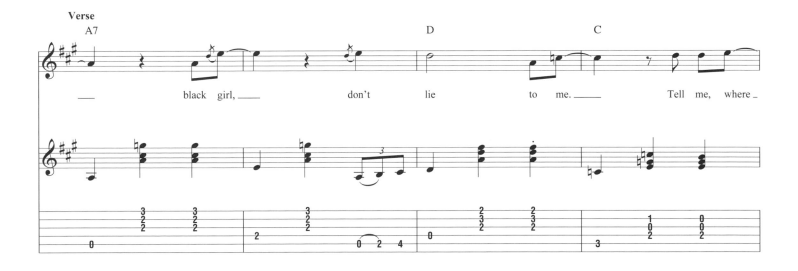

in the pines, __ oh, where the sun nev - er shine. I would shiv-

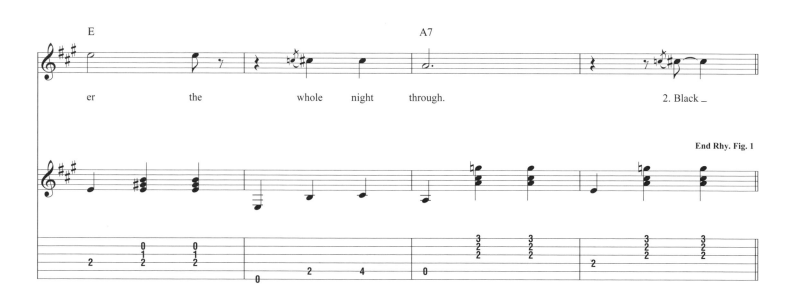

er the whole night through.   2. Black __

Verse

girl, black girl, where __ will _____ you go? _____ I'm go'n' __
girl, black girl, don't lie to me. _____ Tell me,

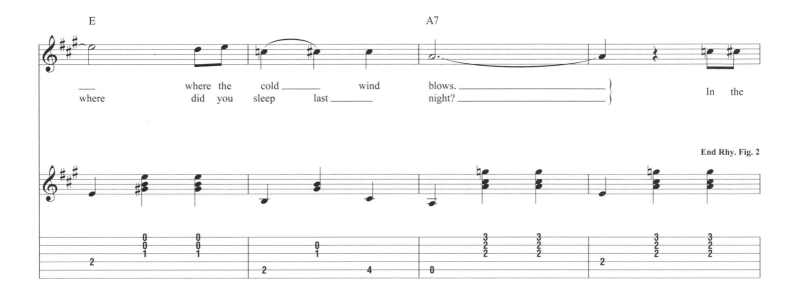

where the cold wind blows. _____

_____ where did you sleep last night? _____ In the

End Rhy. Fig. 2

Gtr. 1: w/ Rhy. Fig. 1

pines, in the pines _____ where the sun nev-er shine. I would shiv-er the

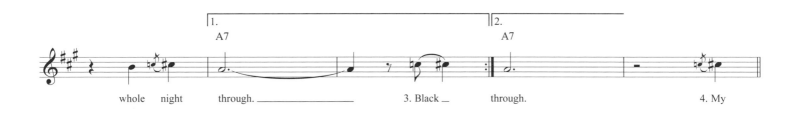

whole night through. _____ 3. Black _____ through. 4. My

Verse

Gtr. 1: w/ Rhy. Fig. 2

hus - band was a rail - road man, killed a

mile and a half _____ from here. _____ His

Gtr. 1: w/ Rhy. Fig. 1 (1st 4 meas.)

head, uh, was found _____ in a driv - er's wheel _____ and his bod -

y have-n't   nev - er   been   found. _____

Gtr. 1

Guitar Solo

5. Black _

Naked as We Came

Words and Music by Sam Beam

Drop D tuning, capo II:
(low to high) D-A-D-G-B-E

Intro
Moderately slow ♩ = 85

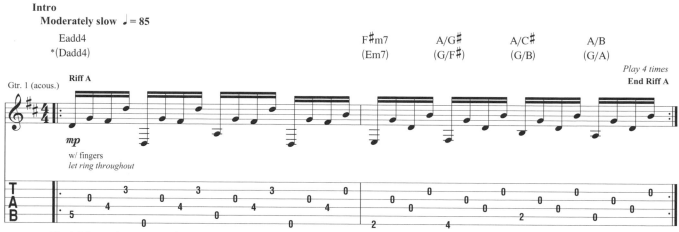

*Symbols in parentheses represent chord names respective to capoed guitar.
Symbols above reflect actual sounding chords. Capoed fret is "0" in tab.
Chord symbols reflect implied harmony.

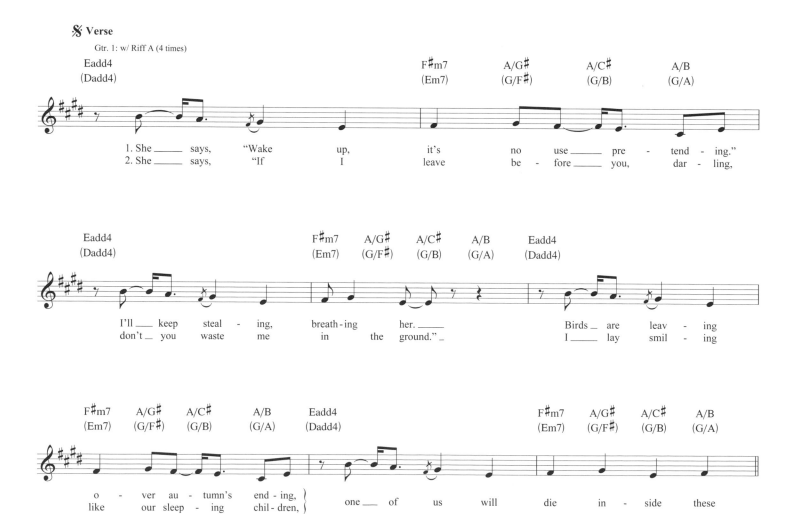

1. She ___ says, "Wake up, it's no use ___ pre - tend - ing."
2. She ___ says, "If I leave be - fore ___ you, dar - ling,

I'll ___ keep steal - ing, breath - ing her. ___
don't ___ you waste me in the ground." ___

Birds ___ are leav - ing
I ___ lay smil - ing

o - ver au - tumn's end - ing,
like our sleep - ing chil - dren,

one ___ of us will die in - side these

Chorus

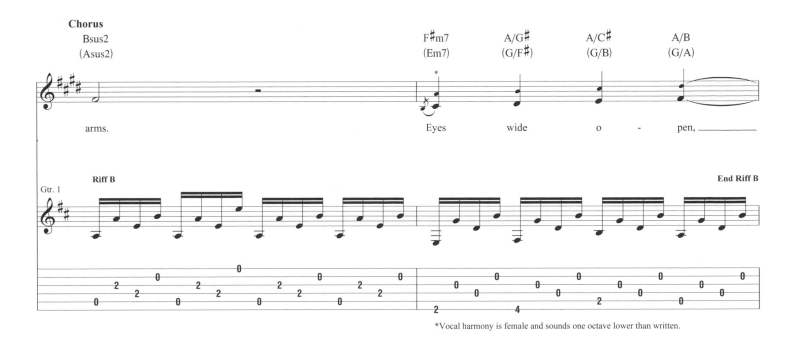

*Vocal harmony is female and sounds one octave lower than written.

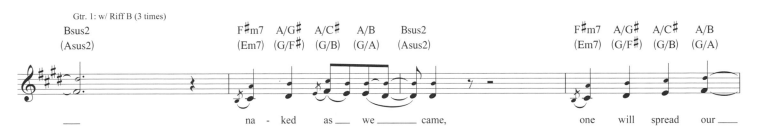

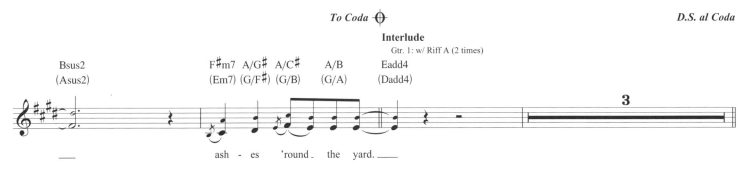

To Coda ⊕

D.S. al Coda

⊕ **Coda**

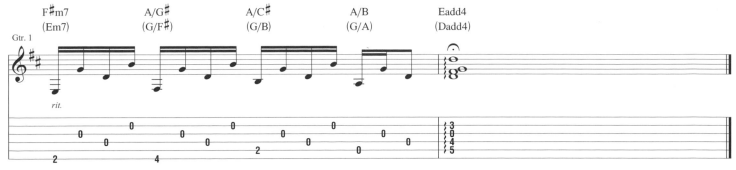

from Gillian Welch - *Revival*

Orphan Girl

Words and Music by Gillian Welch

Gtrs. 1 & 3: Capo I
Gtr. 2: Drop D tuning, capo I

Intro
Moderately ♩ = 120

*Baritone gtr. arr. for standard gtr.   **Symbols in parentheses represent chord names respective to capoed guitar.
Symbols above reflect actual sounding chords. Capoed fret is "0" in tab.

Verse

moth - er,   no fath - er,   no

sis - ter,   no ____ broth - er. ____

I am an or - phan ____ girl.

Rhy. Fig. 2   End Rhy. Fig. 2

Gtr. 1

Gtr. 2

Harm.

Guitar Solo

End Rhy. Fig. 3

3. But when He

Verse
Gtr. 1: w/ Rhy. Fig. 1 (2 times)

calls   me,   I will be a - ble   to meet my

Gtr. 2

fam - 'ly   at God's ____ ta - ble, ____ and I'll meet my ____

girl. I am an or - phan girl.

Pancho & Lefty

Words and Music by Townes Van Zandt

*Symbols in parentheses represent chord names respective to capoed guitar.
Symbols above reflect actual sounding chords. Capoed fret is "0" in tab.
Chord symbols reflect implied harmony.

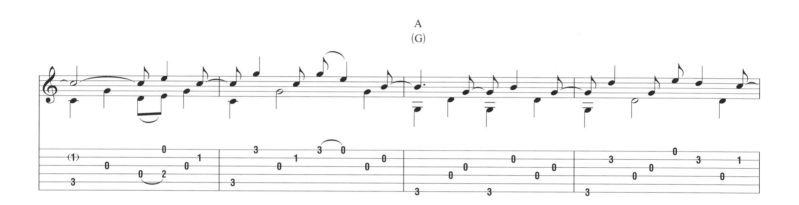

**T = Thumb on 6th string

Verse

1. Liv-ing on ___ the road, ___ my friend, ___ was gon-na keep you free and ___ clean,

now ___ you wear your skin ___ like i - ron, your breath's as hard ___ as ker - o - sene.

You weren't your ma-ma's on - ly boy _ but her fa - v'rite one it seems, _____ she be-gan _

_ to cry _ when you said _____ good - bye, _____

sank in - to your dreams. __

End Riff B

§ Verse

Gtr. 1: w/ Riff A

2. Pan - cho __ was a ban - dit, boys, __ his horse was fast as
3., 4. *See additional lyrics*

Gtr. 2

pol-ished steel, wore his gun out - side ___ his pants ___ for all the hon - est ___ world ___

w/ pick & fingers - - - - ┤

Gtr. 1: w/ Riff B (1st 7 meas.)

___ to feel. ___ Pan - cho ___ met his match, you know, on the des - erts down in

Riff C

Fill 1
Gtr. 2

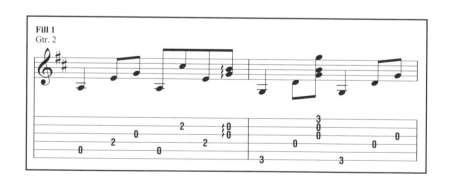

Fill 2
Gtr. 2

any ____ day, ____ they on-ly let him ____ { hang ____ a - round / slip a - way }

D.S. al Coda 1
To Coda 1 ⊕

out of kind - ness, I ____ sup - pose. ____

⊕ **Coda 1**

Fiddle Solo
Gtr. 1: w/ Riff A

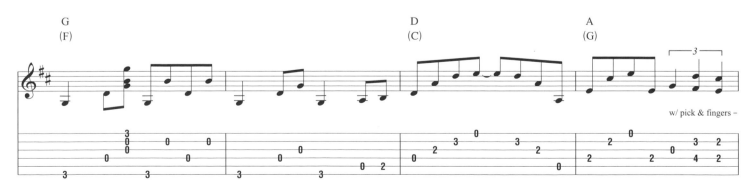

w/ pick & fingers –

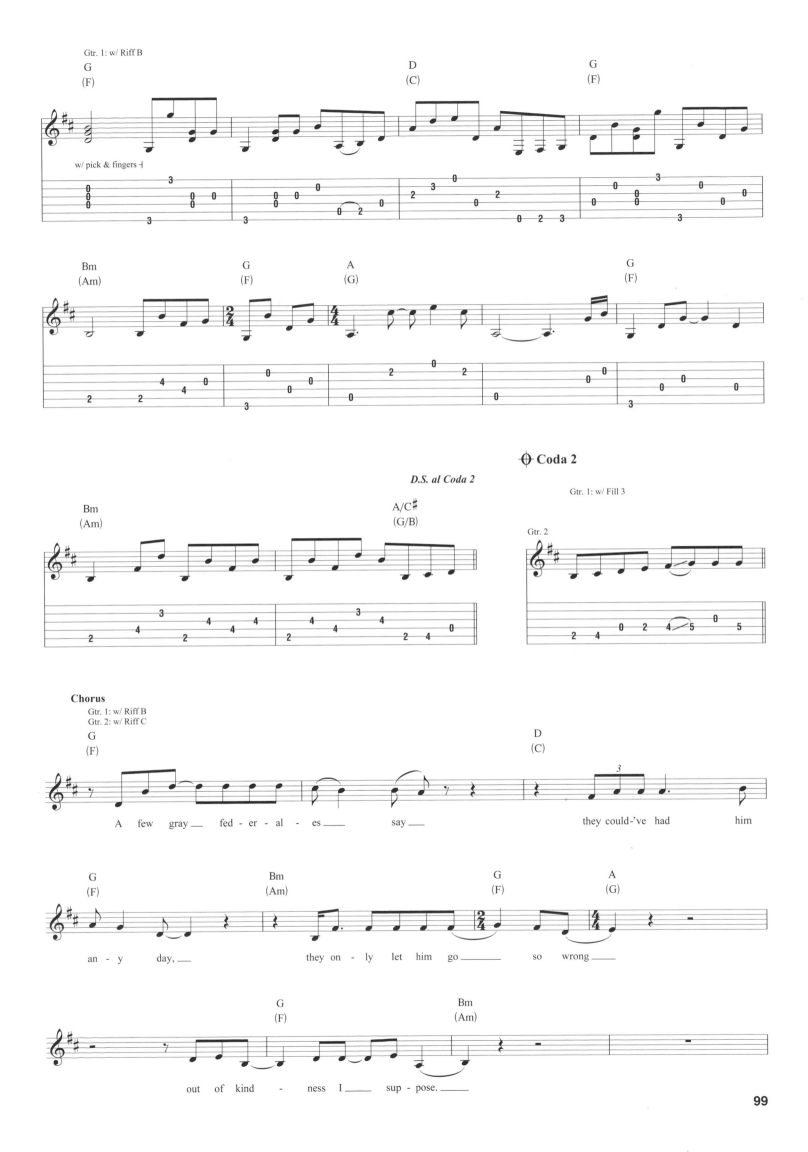

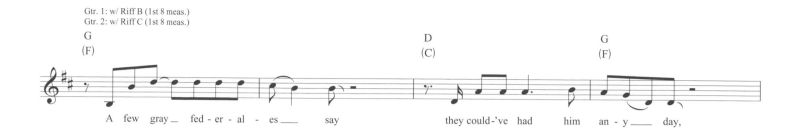

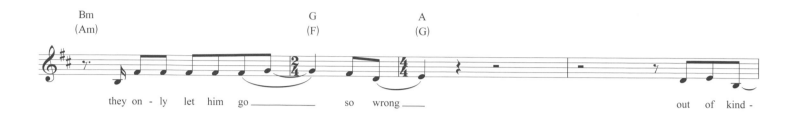

A few gray— fed-er-al-es— say they could-'ve had him an-y— day,

Bm (Am)   G (F)   A (G)

they on-ly let him go— so wrong— out of kind-

-ness I— sup-pose.—

Additional Lyrics

3. Well, Lefty, he can't sing the blues,
   All night long like he used to.
   The dust that Pancho bit down south,
   Ended up in Lefty's mouth.
   The day they laid poor Pancho low,
   Lefty split for Ohio,
   And where he got the bread to go?
   Oh, there ain't nobody knows.

4. When the poets tell how Pancho fell,
   Lefty's living in a cheap hotel.
   The desert's quiet and Cleveland's cold,
   So the story ends, we're told.
   Pancho needs your prayers, it's true,
   But save a few for Lefty too.
   He just did what he had to do,
   Oh, now he's growing old.

Pink Moon

Words and Music by Nick Drake

*Recording sounds 1/4 step sharp.

**Symbols in parentheses represent chord names respective to capoed guitar.
Symbols above reflect actual sounding chords. Capoed fret is "0" in tab.

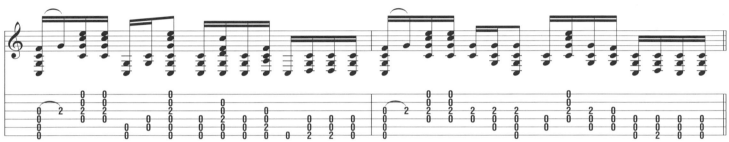

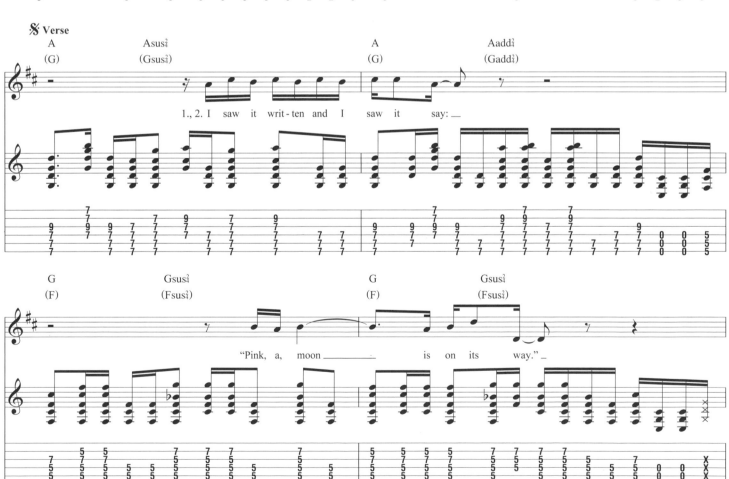

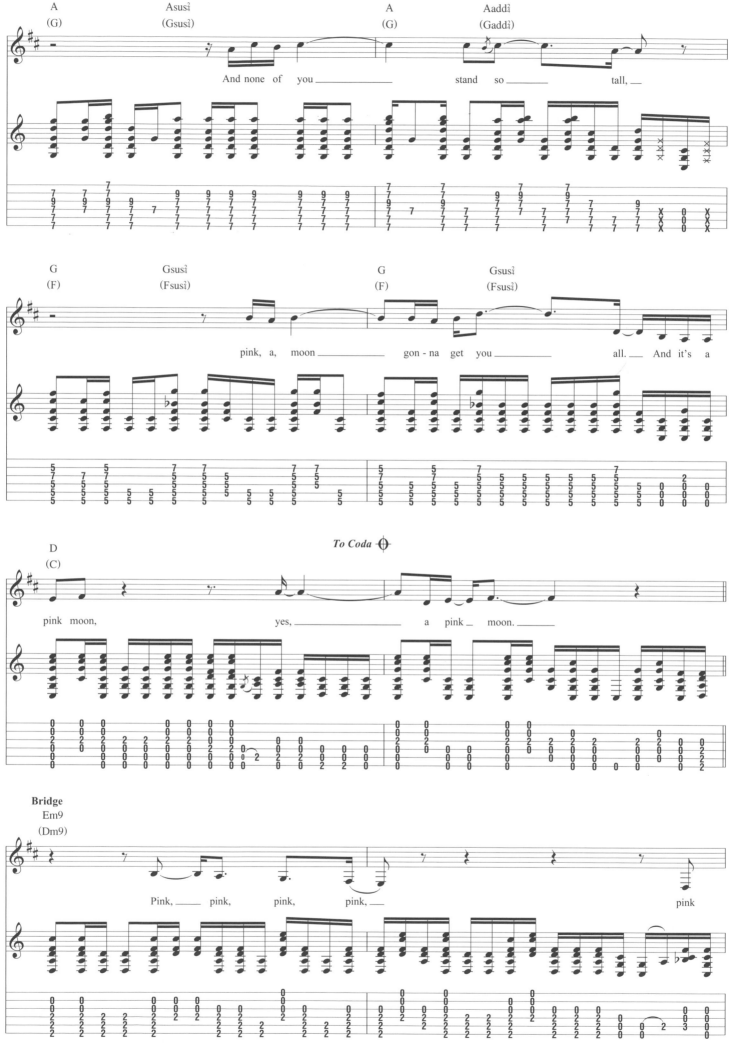

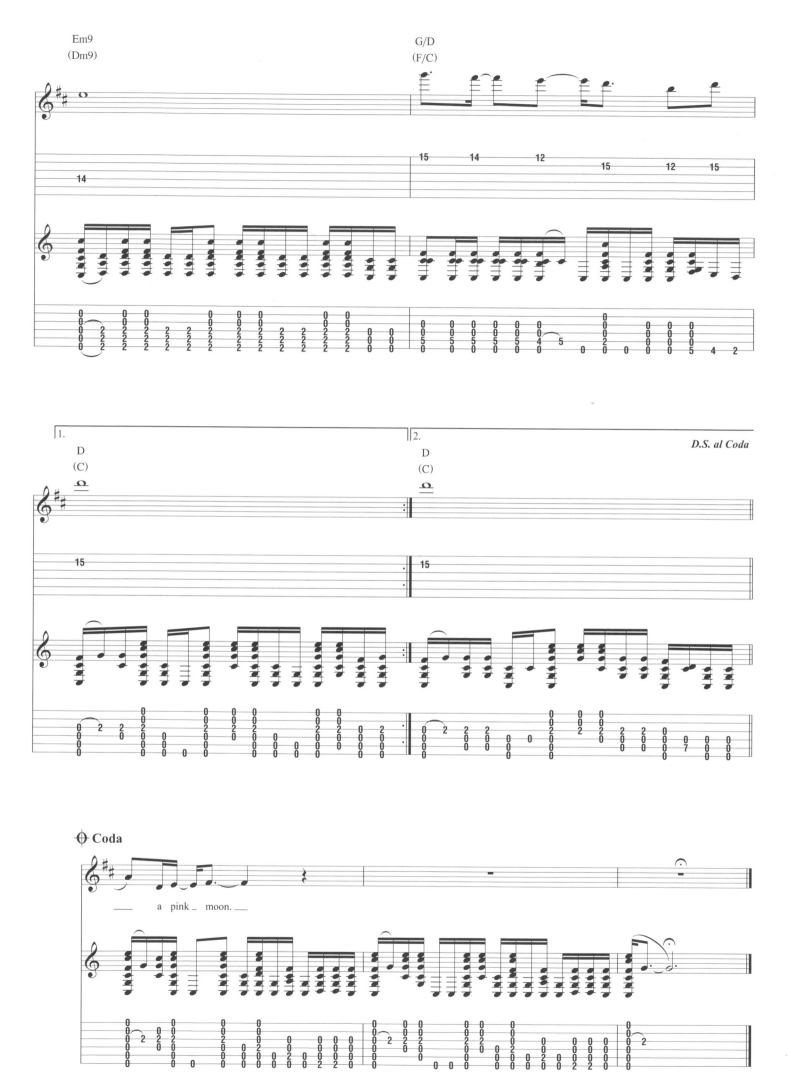

Redemption Song

Words and Music by Bob Marley

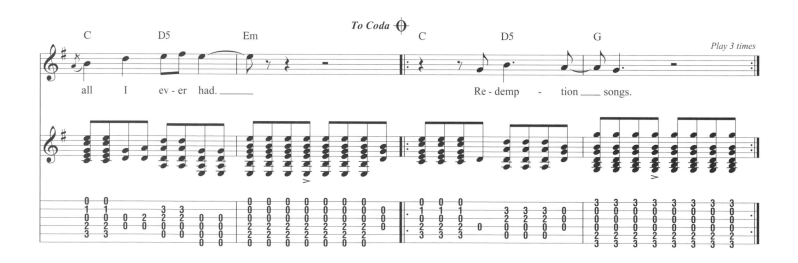

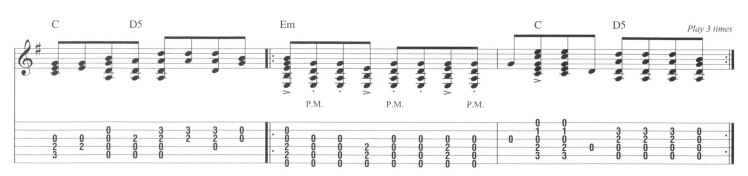

from Grateful Dead - *American Beauty*

Ripple

Words by Robert Hunter
Music by Jerry Garcia

Gtr. 2: Capo VII

Intro
Moderately fast ♩ = 126

*Symbols in parentheses represent chord names respective to capoed guitar.
Symbols above reflect actual sounding chords. Capoed fret is "0" in tab.
Chord symbols reflect implied harmony.

and my tunes ___ were played ___ on the harp, ___ un - strung. ___

*T = Thumb on 6th string

___ Would you hear my voice ___ come through the mu - sic? ___

Would you hold ___ it ___ near, ___ as it were ___ your ___ own? ___

___ 2. It's a hand me down, ___ the thoughts ___ are ___ bro - ken. ___

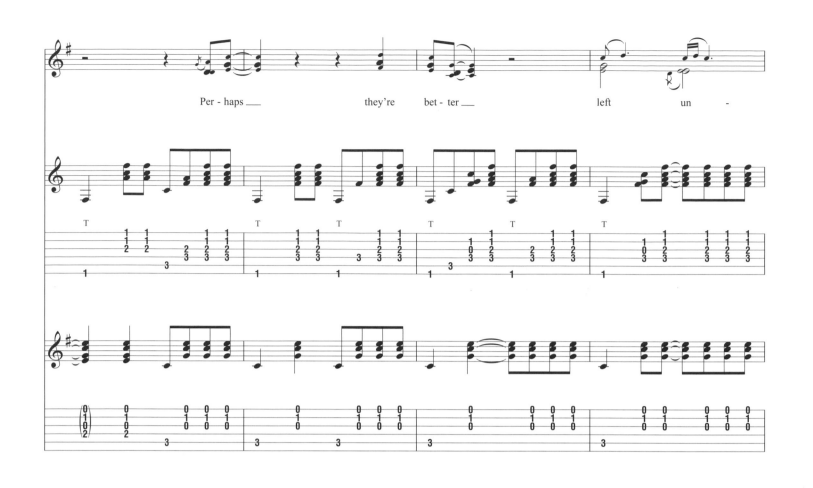

Per - haps ___ they're bet - ter ___ left un -

sung. I don't know ___ don't real - ly care. ___

Let there be songs ___ to fill ___ the air. ___

Chorus

Rip - ple in _____ still ___

wa - ter, ___ when there is ___ no peb - ble tossed. ___ No ___

wind to ___ blow. ___ 3. Reach out ___ your hand, ___ if your cup ___ be ___

emp- ty. If your cup is full, may it be

a - gain. Let it be known, there is a

foun - tain, ___ that was ___ not ___ made ___

Verse

by the hands ___ of man. ___ 4. There is a road, ___ no sim - ple ___

high - way, be - tween the dawn and the dark

of night. And if you go, no one may

fol - low.   That   path   is   for

your   steps   a - lone.

Chorus

Rip - ple in _____ still _____ wa - ter, _____ when there is _____

_____ no _____ peb - ble tossed, _____ no _____ wind to _____ blow. _____ 5. You who choose _____

Verse

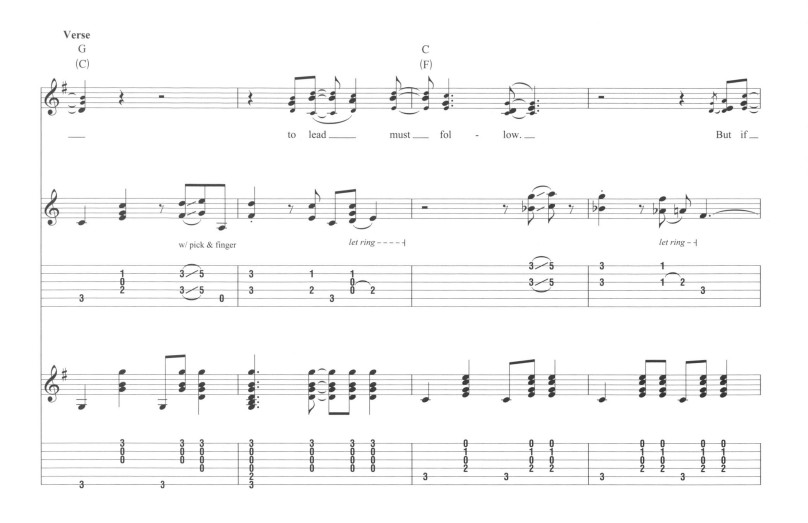

then who's _ to _____ guide you? _

If I knew _ the way, I would take _ you __ home. __ La, n, da, da, da. __

Female: (La, n, da, da, da. __

from Ben Harper - *Diamonds on the Inside*

She's Only Happy in the Sun

Words and Music by Ben Harper and Dean Butterworth

Gtrs. 2 & 3: Capo V

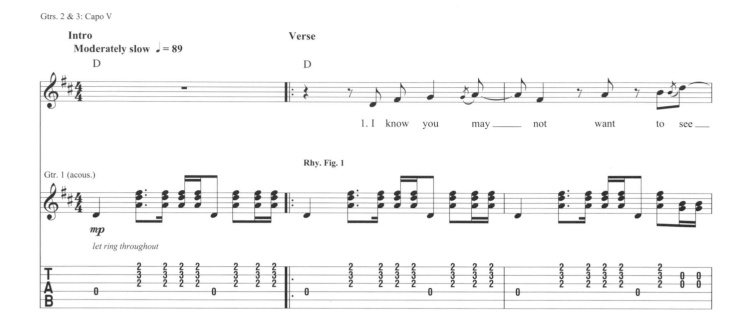

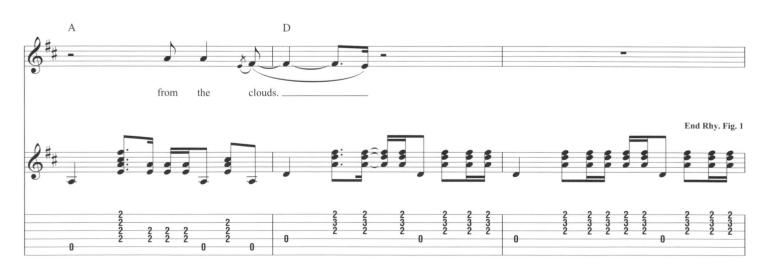

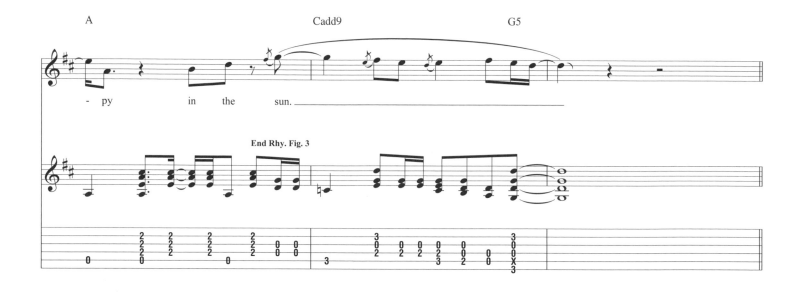

A   Cadd9   G5

-py   in   the   sun.

End Rhy. Fig. 3

Verse

Gtr. 1: w/ Rhy. Fig. 1 (1 3/4 times)

D

2. Did   you   find   what   you   were   af -
3. Ev - 'ry   time   I   hear   you   laugh-

2nd time, Gtr. 2: w/ Fill 1

Em7   G   A
*(Bm7)   (D)   (E)

-ter?   The pain   and the laugh - ter   brought you   to   your
-ing   I hear you   laugh - ing,   it makes me

Gtr. 2 (acous.)

mp
w/ fingers
let ring throughout

*Symbols in parentheses represent chord names respective to capoed guitar.
Symbols above reflect actual sounding chords. Capoed fret is "0" in tab.

Fill 1
Gtr. 2

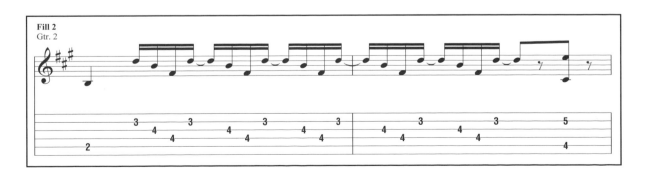

She's on-ly hap - py in the sun.

She's on-ly hap - py in the sun.

Outro-Chorus

Gtr. 1: w/ Rhy. Fig. 3 (1st 4 meas.)
Gtr. 3: w/ Riff A

G
(D)

A
(E)

She's on- ly hap- py in the sun. ___

Gtr. 2

She's on - ly hap - py in the sun. ___

Sportin' Life

Words and Music by John Sebastian, Zal Yanovsky, Joe Butler and Steve Boon

Drop D tuning, capo II:
(low to high) D-A-D-G-B-E

Intro
Moderately slow ♩ = 75

*Symbols in parentheses represent chord names respective to capoed guitar.
Symbols above reflect actual sounding chords. Capoed fret is "0" in tab.
Chord symbols reflect implied harmony.

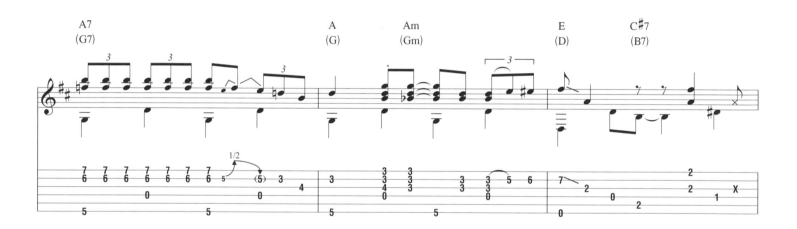

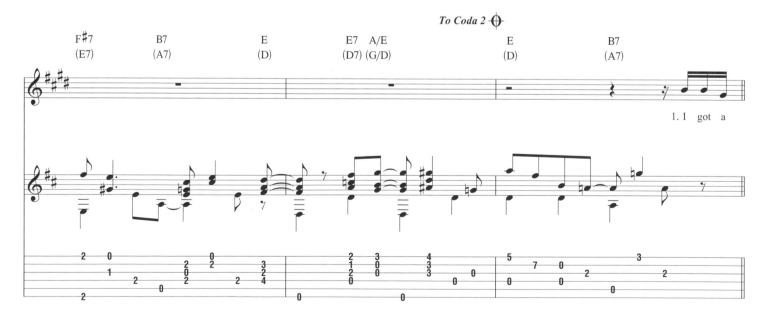

%‌ **Verse**

3rd time, Gtr. 1: w/ Fill 1
4th, 5th & 6th times, Gtr. 1: w/ Fill 2

E7
(D7)

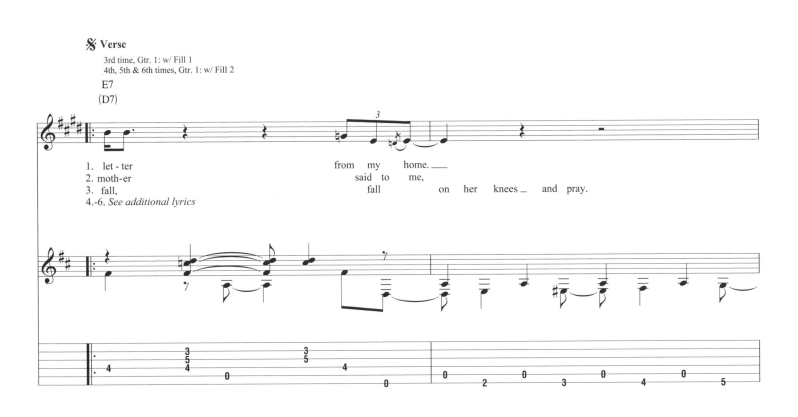

1. let - ter   from   my   home. ___
2. moth-er   said to   me,
3. fall,   fall   on her knees ___ and pray.
4.-6. *See additional lyrics*

A   Am   E
(G)   (Gm)   (D)

Most of my   friends, ___   dead and gone. ___
"You're so young and fool - ish,   child,   you can't   see." I
These   are the ve - ry,   ve - ry words   she'd ___

Fill 1
Gtr. 1

Fill 2
Gtr. 1

It make you wor-ry, / ain't got no moth-er, / — say: "Change, re-ar-range, ___" make you won-der / my sis-ter and my broth-er turned their back on / stop, 'bout times to / stop your low down

1., 2.

To Coda 1

come. / me. / ways."

2. My old ___ / 3. She used to

3.

Guitar Solo

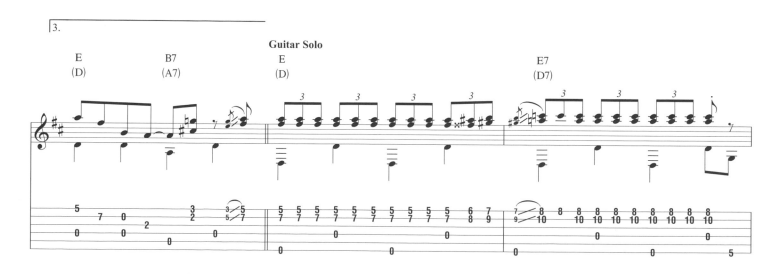

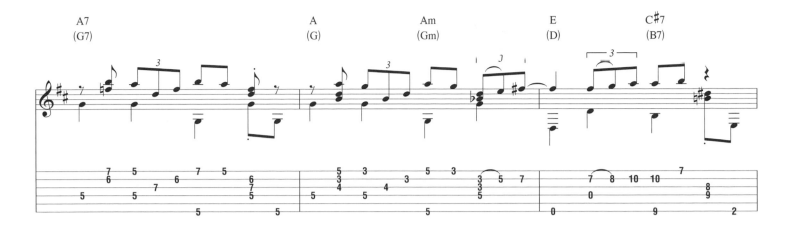

D.S. al Coda 1
(take 1st & 2nd endings)

4. I've been a

✛ **Coda 1**

D.S.S. al Coda 2

✛ **Coda 2**

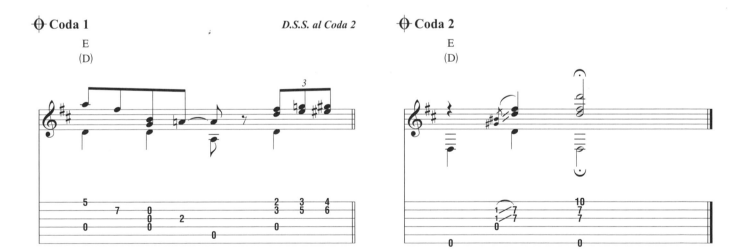

Additional Lyrics

4. I've been a liar, a cheater too.
   I spent my money on booze and you.
   But this old night life, it is a mean life
   And it's killin' me.

5. When I was young and feelin' blue,
   All them young women could see me through.
   Makes you sad, makes you scared,
   Makes you worry what time can do.

6. I'm gettin' tired of runnin' 'round.
   I'm gonna get married, settle down.
   This old night life, this sportin' life
   Is killin' me.

from **The Rolling Stones** - *Exile on Main Street*

Sweet Virginia

Words and Music by Mick Jagger and Keith Richards

Gtr. 1: Capo II

*Symbols in parentheses represent chord names respective to capoed guitar.
Symbols above represent actual sounding chords.
Chord symbols reflect implied harmony.

**T = Thumb on 6th string

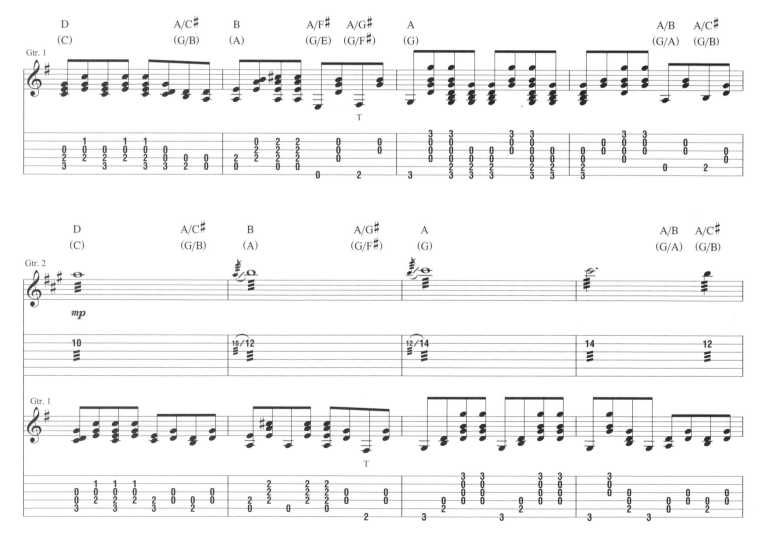

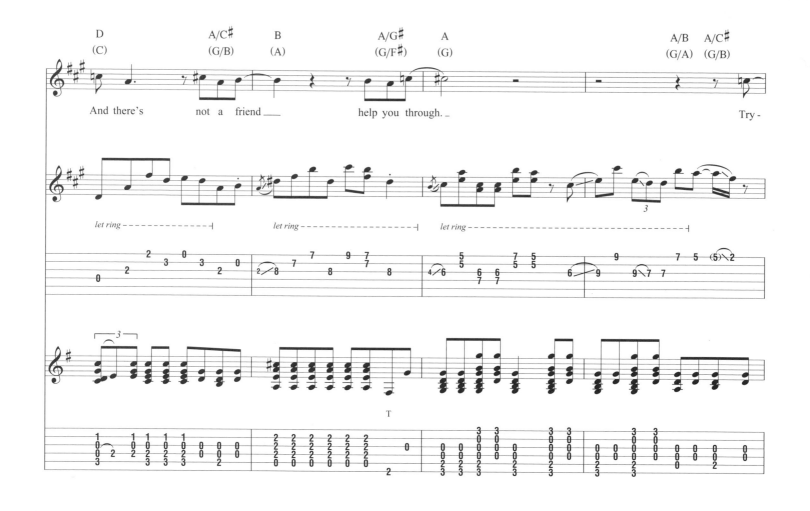

And there's not a friend ___ help you through. ___ Try-

-in' to stop the wave ___ be-hind ___ your eye - balls, ___ uh - huh.

Drop your reds, _ drop your greens _ and blues. _

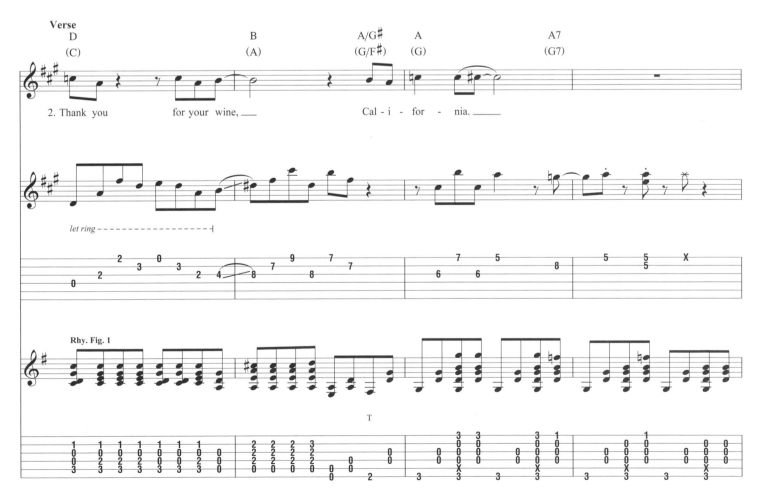

Verse

2. Thank you for your wine, __ Cal - i - for - nia. __

Rhy. Fig. 1

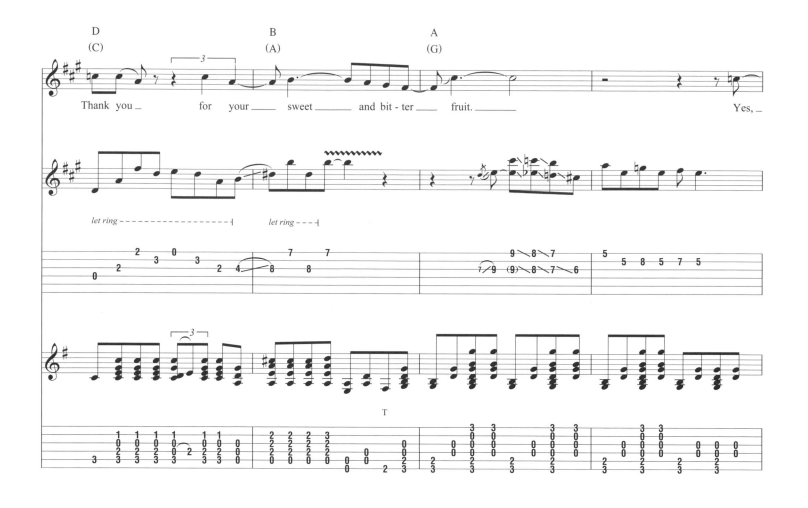

Thank you __ for your __ sweet __ and bit - ter __ fruit. __ Yes, __

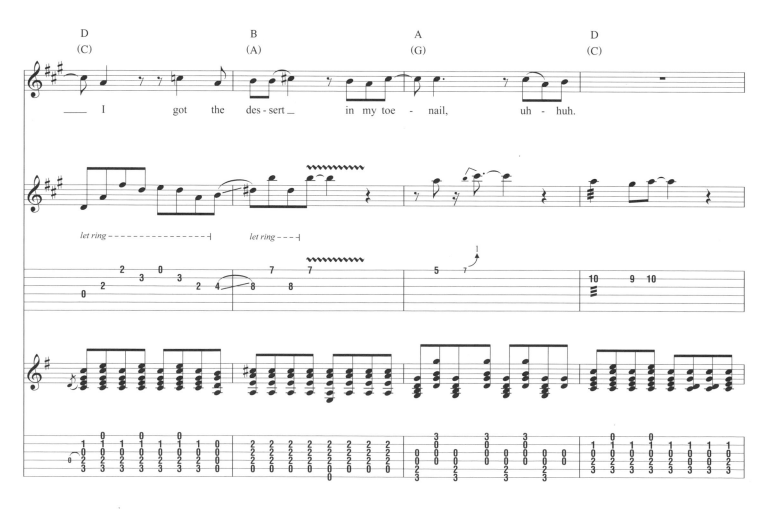

__ I got the des - sert __ in my toe - nail, uh - huh.

on, come on down, you got it in ya. uh-huh.

Got to scrape my shit right off your shoes.

Sax Solo

Gtr. 1: w/ Rhy. Fig. 1

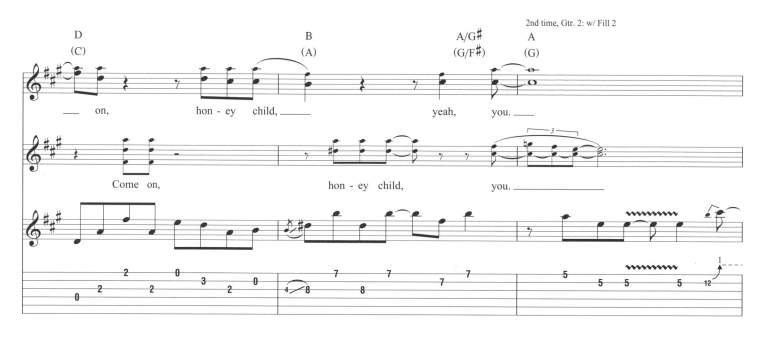

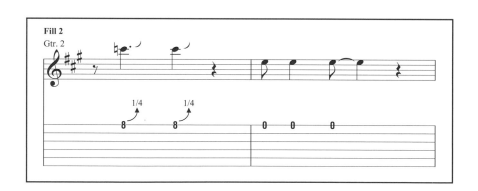

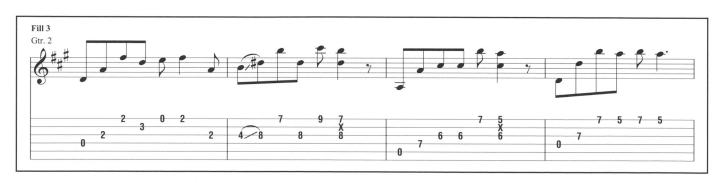

Tennessee Stud

Words and Music by Jimmie Driftwood

Capo V

*Symbols in parentheses represent chord names respective to capoed guitar.
Symbols above reflect actual sounding chords. Capoed fret is "0" in tab.
Chord symbols reflect implied harmony.

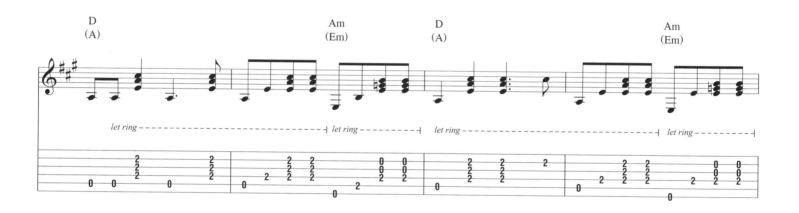

1. A-long a-bout eigh-teen twen-ty - five,__ I left Ten-nes-see ver-y

*Knock on body of guitar w/
pick hand on 3rd downbeat.

Chorus

Gtr. 1: w/ Rhy. Fig. 3

col - or of the sun ___ and his eyes ___ were green. ___

He had the nerve and

he had the blood, and there nev - er was a horse ___ like the Ten - nes - see Stud. ___

Interlude

Gtr. 1: w/ Riff A

Coda

Outro

Gtr. 1

Urge for Going

Words and Music by Joni Mitchell

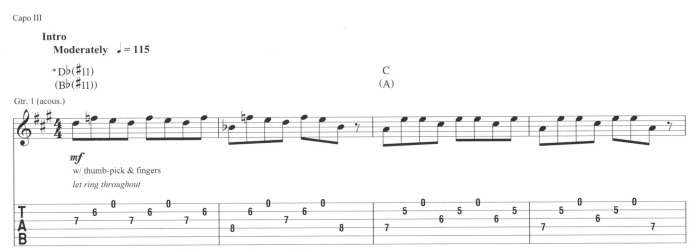

*Symbols in parentheses represent chord names respective to capoed guitar.
Symbols above reflect actual sounding chords. Capoed fret is "0" in tab.
Chord symbols reflect implied harmony.

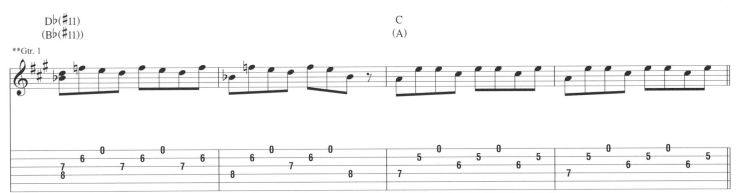

**Two gtrs. arr. for one.

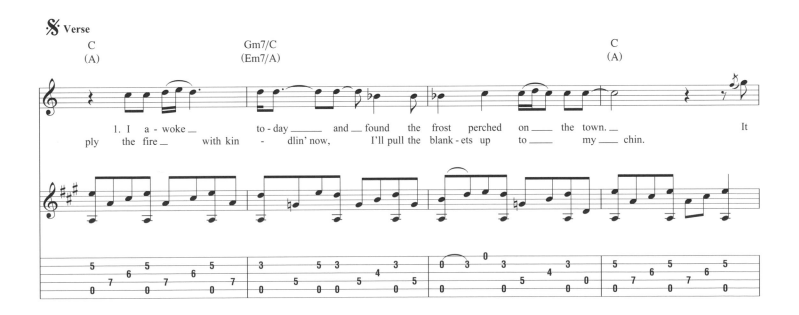

from The Carter Family - *RCA Country Legends*

Wildwood Flower

Words and Music by A.P. Carter

Tune down 1 1/2 steps:
(low to high) C#-F#-B-E-G#-C#

Intro
Moderately ♩ = 108

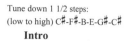

*Chord symbols reflect implied harmony.

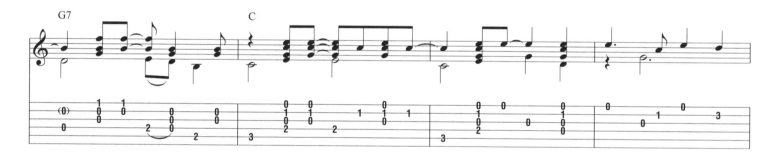

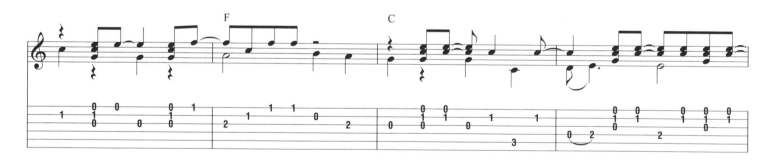

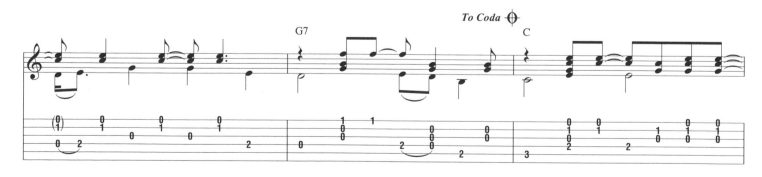

Verse

2nd time, Gtr. 1: w/ Fill 1
4th time, Gtr. 1: w/ Fill 2

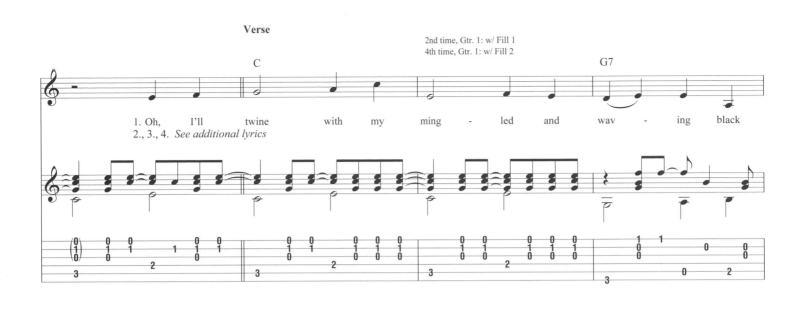

1. Oh, I'll twine with my ming - led and wav - ing black
2., 3., 4. *See additional lyrics*

2nd & 4th time, Gtr. 1: w/ Fill 2

hair, with the ros - es so red and the

lil - ies so fair. And the myr - tle so

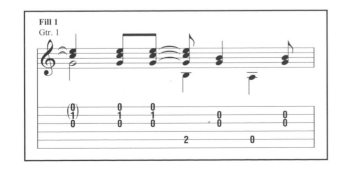

Fill 1
Gtr. 1

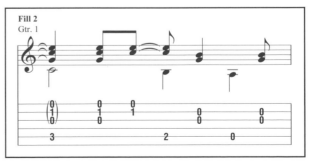

Fill 2
Gtr. 1

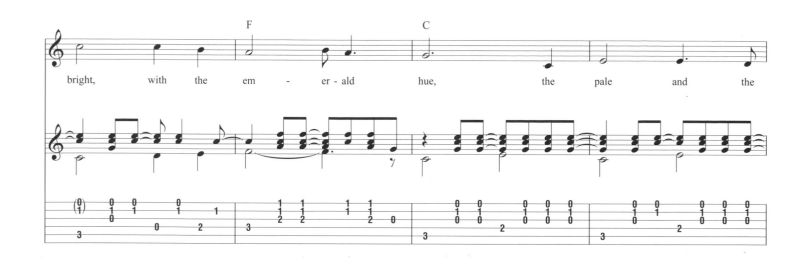

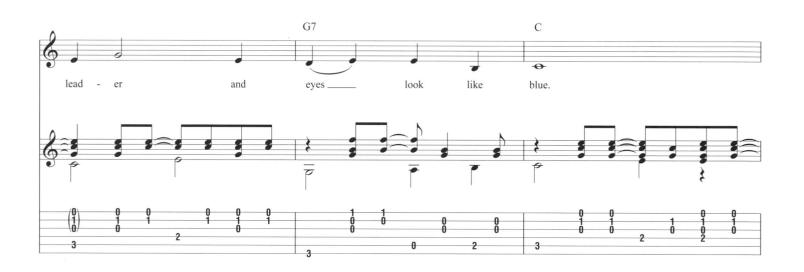

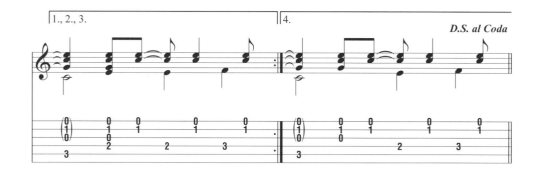

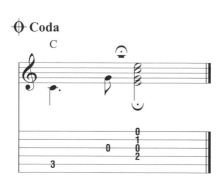

Additional Lyrics

2. I will dance, I will sing and my life shall be gay.
   I will charm ev'ry heart, in his crown I will sway.
   When I woke from dreaming, my idols was clay.
   All portion of love had all flown away.

3. Oh, he taught me to love him and promised to love,
   And to cherish me over all others above.
   How my heart is now wond'ring, no misery can tell.
   He's left me no warning, no words of farewell.

4. Oh, he taught me to love him and called me his flower,
   That's blooming to cheer him through life's dreary hour.
   Oh, I long to see him and regret the dark hour.
   He's won and neglected this pale wildwood flower.

GUITAR NOTATION LEGEND

Guitar music can be notated three different ways: on a *musical staff*, in *tablature*, and in *rhythm slashes*.

RHYTHM SLASHES are written above the staff. Strum chords in the rhythm indicated. Use the chord diagrams found at the top of the first page of the transcription for the appropriate chord voicings. Round noteheads indicate single notes.

THE MUSICAL STAFF shows pitches and rhythms and is divided by bar lines into measures. Pitches are named after the first seven letters of the alphabet.

TABLATURE graphically represents the guitar fingerboard. Each horizontal line represents a string, and each number represents a fret.

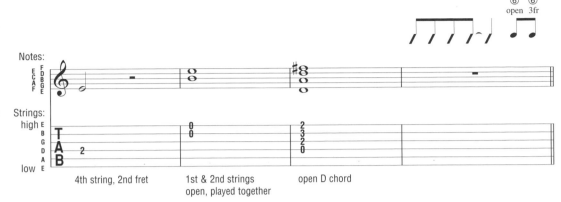

4th string, 2nd fret

1st & 2nd strings open, played together

open D chord

Definitions for Special Guitar Notation

HALF-STEP BEND: Strike the note and bend up 1/2 step.

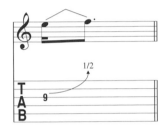

WHOLE-STEP BEND: Strike the note and bend up one step.

GRACE NOTE BEND: Strike the note and immediately bend up as indicated.

SLIGHT (MICROTONE) BEND: Strike the note and bend up 1/4 step.

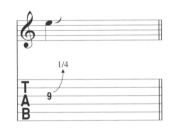

BEND AND RELEASE: Strike the note and bend up as indicated, then release back to the original note. Only the first note is struck.

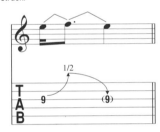

PRE-BEND: Bend the note as indicated, then strike it.

PRE-BEND AND RELEASE: Bend the note as indicated. Strike it and release the bend back to the original note.

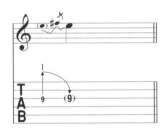

UNISON BEND: Strike the two notes simultaneously and bend the lower note up to the pitch of the higher.

VIBRATO: The string is vibrated by rapidly bending and releasing the note with the fretting hand.

WIDE VIBRATO: The pitch is varied to a greater degree by vibrating with the fretting hand.

HAMMER-ON: Strike the first (lower) note with one finger, then sound the higher note (on the same string) with another finger by fretting it without picking.

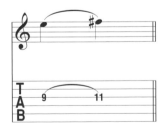

PULL-OFF: Place both fingers on the notes to be sounded. Strike the first note and without picking, pull the finger off to sound the second (lower) note.

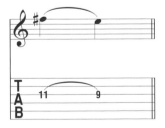

LEGATO SLIDE: Strike the first note and then slide the same fret-hand finger up or down to the second note. The second note is not struck.

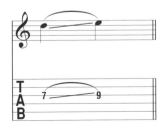

SHIFT SLIDE: Same as legato slide, except the second note is struck.

TRILL: Very rapidly alternate between the notes indicated by continuously hammering on and pulling off.

TAPPING: Hammer ("tap") the fret indicated with the pick-hand index or middle finger and pull off to the note fretted by the fret hand.

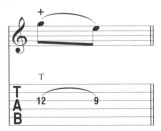

NATURAL HARMONIC: Strike the note while the fret-hand lightly touches the string directly over the fret indicated.

Harm.

TAB 12

PINCH HARMONIC: The note is fretted normally and a harmonic is produced by adding the edge of the thumb or the tip of the index finger of the pick hand to the normal pick attack.

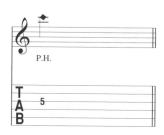

P.H.

TAB 5

HARP HARMONIC: The note is fretted normally and a harmonic is produced by gently resting the pick hand's index finger directly above the indicated fret (in parentheses) while the pick hand's thumb or pick assists by plucking the appropriate string.

8va - - - ┐

H.H.

TAB 7⟨19⟩

PICK SCRAPE: The edge of the pick is rubbed down (or up) the string, producing a scratchy sound.

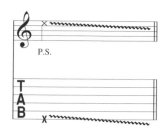

P.S.

MUFFLED STRINGS: A percussive sound is produced by laying the fret hand across the string(s) without depressing, and striking them with the pick hand.

TAB X X

PALM MUTING: The note is partially muted by the pick hand lightly touching the string(s) just before the bridge.

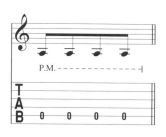

P.M. - - - - - - - - - - - - ┤

TAB 0 0 0 0

RAKE: Drag the pick across the strings indicated with a single motion.

rake - - ┤

TAB 5 X X

TREMOLO PICKING: The note is picked as rapidly and continuously as possible.

TAB 5 7

ARPEGGIATE: Play the notes of the chord indicated by quickly rolling them from bottom to top.

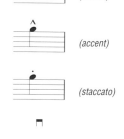

TAB 5 5 5 5

VIBRATO BAR DIVE AND RETURN: The pitch of the note or chord is dropped a specified number of steps (in rhythm), then returned to the original pitch.

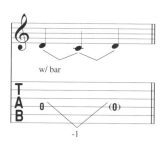

w/ bar

TAB 0 (0)
-1

VIBRATO BAR SCOOP: Depress the bar just before striking the note, then quickly release the bar.

w/ bar - - - - - - - - - ┤

TAB 4 5 7

VIBRATO BAR DIP: Strike the note and then immediately drop a specified number of steps, then release back to the original pitch.

-1/2   -1/2   -1/2

w/ bar - - - - - - - - - - ┤

-1/2   -1/2   -1/2

TAB 7 7 7

Additional Musical Definitions

(accent)	• Accentuate note (play it louder).	
(accent)	• Accentuate note with great intensity.	
(staccato)	• Play the note short.	
⊓	• Downstroke	
V	• Upstroke	
D.S. al Coda	• Go back to the sign (%), then play until the measure marked "*To Coda*," then skip to the section labelled "**Coda**."	
D.C. al Fine	• Go back to the beginning of the song and play until the measure marked "*Fine*" (end).	

Rhy. Fig. • Label used to recall a recurring accompaniment pattern (usually chordal).

Riff • Label used to recall composed, melodic lines (usually single notes) which recur.

Fill • Label used to identify a brief melodic figure which is to be inserted into the arrangement.

Rhy. Fill • A chordal version of a Fill.

tacet • Instrument is silent (drops out).

• Repeat measures between signs.

• When a repeated section has different endings, play the first ending only the first time and the second ending only the second time.

NOTE: Tablature numbers in parentheses mean:
1. The note is being sustained over a system (note in standard notation is tied), or
2. The note is sustained, but a new articulation (such as a hammer-on, pull-off, slide or vibrato) begins, or
3. The note is a barely audible "ghost" note (note in standard notation is also in parentheses).

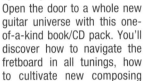 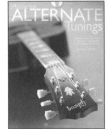
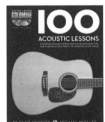

GUITAR RECORDED VERSIONS®

Guitar Recorded Versions® are note-for-note transcriptions of guitar music taken directly off recordings. This series, one of the most popular in print today, features some of the greatest guitar players and groups from blues and rock to country and jazz.

Guitar Recorded Versions are transcribed by the best transcribers in the business. Every book contains notes and tablature. Visit **www.halleonard.com** for our complete selection.

AUTHENTIC TRANSCRIPTIONS WITH NOTES AND TABLATURE

00690169	Eric Johnson – Venus Isle	$22.95
00122439	Jack Johnson – From Here to Now to You	$22.99
00690846	Jack Johnson and Friends – Sing A Longs and Lullabies for the Film Curious George	$19.95
00690271	Robert Johnson – The New Transcriptions	$24.95
00699131	Best of Janis Joplin	$19.95
00690427	Best of Judas Priest	$22.99
00690277	Best of Kansas	$19.95
00690911	Best of Phil Keaggy	$24.99
00690727	Toby Keith Guitar Collection	$19.99
00120814	Killswitch Engage – Disarm the Descent	$22.99
00690504	Very Best of Albert King	$19.95
00690444	B.B. King & Eric Clapton – Riding with the King	$22.99
00690134	Freddie King Collection	$19.95
00691062	Kings of Leon – Come Around Sundown	$22.99
00690157	Kiss – Alive!	$19.95
00690356	Kiss – Alive II	$22.99
00694903	Best of Kiss for Guitar	$24.95
00690355	Kiss – Destroyer	$16.95
14026320	Mark Knopfler – Get Lucky	$22.99
00690164	Mark Knopfler Guitar – Vol. 1	$19.95
00690163	Mark Knopfler/Chet Atkins – Neck and Neck	$19.95
00690780	Korn – Greatest Hits, Volume 1	$22.95
00690377	Kris Kristofferson Collection	$19.95
00690834	Lamb of God – Ashes of the Wake	$19.95
00690875	Lamb of God – Sacrament	$19.95
00690977	Ray LaMontagne – Gossip in the Grain	$19.99
00690823	Ray LaMontagne – Trouble	$19.95
00691057	Ray LaMontagne and the Pariah Dogs – God Willin' & The Creek Don't Rise	$22.99
00690781	Linkin Park – Hybrid Theory	$22.95
00690782	Linkin Park – Meteora	$22.95
00690922	Linkin Park – Minutes to Midnight	$19.95
00699623	The Best of Chuck Loeb	$19.95
00114563	The Lumineers	$22.99
00690525	Best of George Lynch	$24.99
00690955	Lynyrd Skynyrd – All-Time Greatest Hits	$19.99
00694954	New Best of Lynyrd Skynyrd	$19.95
00690577	Yngwie Malmsteen – Anthology	$24.95
00690754	Marilyn Manson – Lest We Forget	$19.95
00694956	Bob Marley – Legend	$19.95
00690548	Very Best of Bob Marley & The Wailers – One Love	$22.99
00694945	Bob Marley – Songs of Freedom	$24.95
00690914	Maroon 5 – It Won't Be Soon Before Long	$19.95
00690657	Maroon 5 – Songs About Jane	$19.95
00690748	Maroon 5 – 1.22.03 Acoustic	$19.95
00690989	Mastodon – Crack the Skye	$22.99
00119220	Brent Mason – Hot Wired	$19.99
00691176	Mastodon – The Hunter	$22.99
00137718	Mastodon – Once More 'Round the Sun	$22.99
00690616	Matchbox Twenty – More Than You Think You Are	$19.95
00690239	Matchbox 20 – Yourself or Someone like You	$19.95
00691942	Andy McKee – Art of Motion	$22.99
00691034	Andy McKee – Joyland	$19.99
00120080	The Don McLean Songbook	$19.95
00694952	Megadeth – Countdown to Extinction	$22.95
00690244	Megadeth – Cryptic Writings	$19.95
00694951	Megadeth – Rust in Peace	$22.95
00690011	Megadeth – Youthanasia	$19.95
00690505	John Mellencamp Guitar Collection	$19.95
00690562	Pat Metheny – Bright Size Life	$19.95
00691073	Pat Metheny with Christian McBride & Antonion Sanchez – Day Trip/Tokyo Day Trip Live	$22.99
00690646	Pat Metheny – One Quiet Night	$19.95
00690559	Pat Metheny – Question & Answer	$19.95
00118836	Pat Metheny – Unity Band	$22.99
00102590	Pat Metheny – What's It All About	$22.99
00690040	Steve Miller Band Greatest Hits	$19.95
00119338	Ministry Guitar Tab Collection	$24.99
00690769	Modest Mouse – Good News for People Who Love Bad News	$19.95
00102591	Wes Montgomery Guitar Anthology	$24.99
00694802	Gary Moore – Still Got the Blues	$22.99
00691005	Best of Motion City Soundtrack	$19.99
00690787	Mudvayne – L.D. 50	$22.95
00691070	Mumford & Sons – Sigh No More	$22.99
00118196	Muse – The 2nd Law	$19.99
00690996	My Morning Jacket Collection	$19.99
00690984	Matt Nathanson – Some Mad Hope	$22.99
00690611	Nirvana	$22.95
00694895	Nirvana – Bleach	$19.95
00694913	Nirvana – In Utero	$19.95
00694883	Nirvana – Nevermind	$19.95
00690026	Nirvana – Unplugged in New York	$19.95
00120112	No Doubt – Tragic Kingdom	$22.95
00690226	Oasis – The Other Side of Oasis	$19.95
00307163	Oasis – Time Flies... 1994-2009	$19.99
00690818	The Best of Opeth	$22.95
00691052	Roy Orbison – Black & White Night	$22.99
00694847	Best of Ozzy Osbourne	$22.95
00690399	Ozzy Osbourne – The Ozzman Cometh	$22.99
00690129	Ozzy Osbourne – Ozzmosis	$22.95
00690933	Best of Brad Paisley	$22.95
00690995	Brad Paisley – Play: The Guitar Album	$24.99
00690939	Christopher Parkening – Solo Pieces	$19.99
00690594	Best of Les Paul	$19.95
00694855	Pearl Jam – Ten	$22.99
00690439	A Perfect Circle – Mer De Noms	$19.95
00690725	Best of Carl Perkins	$19.99
00690499	Tom Petty – Definitive Guitar Collection	$19.95
00690868	Tom Petty – Highway Companion	$19.95
00690176	Phish – Billy Breathes	$22.95
00691249	Phish – Junta	$22.99
00690428	Pink Floyd – Dark Side of the Moon	$19.95
00690789	Best of Poison	$19.95
00690299	Best of Elvis: The King of Rock 'n' Roll	$19.95
00692535	Elvis Presley	$19.95
00690925	The Very Best of Prince	$22.99
00690003	Classic Queen	$24.95
00694975	Queen – Greatest Hits	$24.95
00690670	Very Best of Queensryche	$19.95
00690878	The Raconteurs – Broken Boy Soldiers	$19.95
00109303	Radiohead Guitar Anthology	$24.99
00694910	Rage Against the Machine	$19.95
00119834	Rage Against the Machine – Guitar Anthology	$22.99
00690179	Rancid – And Out Come the Wolves	$22.95
00690426	Best of Ratt	$19.95
00690055	Red Hot Chili Peppers – Blood Sugar Sex Magik	$19.95
00690584	Red Hot Chili Peppers – By the Way	$19.95
00690379	Red Hot Chili Peppers – Californication	$19.95
00690673	Red Hot Chili Peppers – Greatest Hits	$19.95
00690090	Red Hot Chili Peppers – One Hot Minute	$22.95
00691166	Red Hot Chili Peppers – I'm with You	$22.99
00690852	Red Hot Chili Peppers – Stadium Arcadium	$24.95
00690511	Django Reinhardt – The Definitive Collection	$19.95
00690779	Relient K – MMHMM	$19.95
00690643	Relient K – Two Lefts Don't Make a Right ... But Three Do	$19.95
00690260	Jimmie Rodgers Guitar Collection	$19.95
14041901	Rodrigo Y Gabriela and C.U.B.A. – Area 52	$24.99
00690014	Rolling Stones – Exile on Main Street	$24.95
00690631	Rolling Stones – Guitar Anthology	$27.95
00690685	David Lee Roth – Eat 'Em and Smile	$19.95
00690031	Santana's Greatest Hits	$19.95
00690796	Very Best of Michael Schenker	$19.95
00690566	Best of Scorpions	$22.95
00690604	Bob Seger – Guitar Anthology	$22.99
00691012	Shadows Fall – Retribution	$22.99
00690803	Best of Kenny Wayne Shepherd Band	$19.95
00690750	Kenny Wayne Shepherd – The Place You're In	$19.95
00690857	Shinedown – Us and Them	$19.95
00122218	Skillet – Rise	$22.99
00690872	Slayer – Christ Illusion	$19.95
00690813	Slayer – Guitar Collection	$19.95
00690419	Slipknot	$19.95
00690973	Slipknot – All Hope Is Gone	$22.99
00690330	Social Distortion – Live at the Roxy	$19.95
00120004	Best of Steely Dan	$24.95
00694921	Best of Steppenwolf	$22.95
00690655	Best of Mike Stern	$19.95
14041588	Cat Stevens – Tea for the Tillerman	$19.99
00690949	Rod Stewart Guitar Anthology	$19.99
00690021	Sting – Fields of Gold	$19.95
00690520	Styx Guitar Collection	$19.95
00120081	Sublime	$19.95
00690992	Sublime – Robbin' the Hood	$19.99
00690519	SUM 41 – All Killer No Filler	$19.95
00691072	Best of Supertramp	$22.99
00690994	Taylor Swift	$22.99
00690993	Taylor Swift – Fearless	$22.99
00115957	Taylor Swift – Red	$21.99
00691063	Taylor Swift – Speak Now	$22.99
00690767	Switchfoot – The Beautiful Letdown	$19.95
00690531	System of a Down – Toxicity	$19.95

RECORDED VERSIONS GUITAR®

AUTHENTIC TRANSCRIPTIONS WITH NOTES AND TABLATURE

00694824	Best of James Taylor	$17.99
00694887	Best of Thin Lizzy	$19.95
00690871	Three Days Grace – One-X	$19.95
00690891	30 Seconds to Mars – A Beautiful Lie	$19.95
00690233	The Merle Travis Collection	$19.99
00690683	Robin Trower – Bridge of Sighs	$19.95
00699191	U2 – Best of: 1980-1990	$19.95
00690732	U2 – Best of: 1990-2000	$19.95
00690894	U2 – 18 Singles	$19.95
00690039	Steve Vai – Alien Love Secrets	$24.95
00690172	Steve Vai – Fire Garden	$24.95
00660137	Steve Vai – Passion & Warfare	$24.95
00690881	Steve Vai – Real Illusions: Reflections	$24.95
00694904	Steve Vai – Sex and Religion	$24.95
00110385	Steve Vai – The Story of Light	$22.99
00690392	Steve Vai – The Ultra Zone	$19.95
00700555	Van Halen – Van Halen	$19.99
00690024	Stevie Ray Vaughan – Couldn't Stand the Weather	$19.95
00690370	Stevie Ray Vaughan and Double Trouble – The Real Deal: Greatest Hits Volume 2	$22.95
00690116	Stevie Ray Vaughan – Guitar Collection	$24.95
00660136	Stevie Ray Vaughan – In Step	$19.95
00694879	Stevie Ray Vaughan – In the Beginning	$19.95
00660058	Stevie Ray Vaughan – Lightnin' Blues '83-'87	$24.95
00690036	Stevie Ray Vaughan – Live Alive	$24.95
00694835	Stevie Ray Vaughan – The Sky Is Crying	$22.95
00690025	Stevie Ray Vaughan – Soul to Soul	$19.95
00690015	Stevie Ray Vaughan – Texas Flood	$19.95
00690772	Velvet Revolver – Contraband	$22.95
00109770	Volbeat Guitar Collection	$22.99
00121808	Volbeat – Outlaw Gentlemen & Shady Ladies	$22.99
00690132	The T-Bone Walker Collection	$19.95
00694789	Muddy Waters – Deep Blues	$24.95
00690071	Weezer (The Blue Album)	$19.95
00690516	Weezer (The Green Album)	$19.95
00690286	Weezer – Pinkerton	$19.95
00691046	Weezer – Rarities Edition	$22.99
00117511	Whitesnake Guitar Collection	$19.99
00690447	Best of the Who	$24.95
00691941	The Who – Acoustic Guitar Collection	$22.99
00691006	Wilco Guitar Collection	$22.99
00690672	Best of Dar Williams	$19.95
00691017	Wolfmother – Cosmic Egg	$22.99
00690319	Stevie Wonder – Some of the Best	$17.95
00690596	Best of the Yardbirds	$19.95
00690844	Yellowcard – Lights and Sounds	$19.95
00690916	The Best of Dwight Yoakam	$19.95
00691020	Neil Young – After the Goldrush	$22.99
00691019	Neil Young – Everybody Knows This Is Nowhere	$19.99
00690904	Neil Young – Harvest	$29.99
00691021	Neil Young – Harvest Moon	$22.99
00690905	Neil Young – Rust Never Sleeps	$19.99
00690443	Frank Zappa – Hot Rats	$19.95
00690624	Frank Zappa and the Mothers of Invention – One Size Fits All	$22.99
00690623	Frank Zappa – Over-Nite Sensation	$22.99
00121684	ZZ Top – Early Classics	$24.99
00690589	ZZ Top – Guitar Anthology	$24.95
00690960	ZZ Top Guitar Classics	$19.99

HAL•LEONARD® CORPORATION

7777 W. Bluemound Rd. P.O. Box 13819 Milwaukee, WI 53213

Complete songlists and more at **www.halleonard.com**

Prices, contents, and availability subject to change without notice.

1214

GUITAR *signature licks*

Signature Licks book/CD packs provide a step-by-step breakdown of "right from the record" riffs, licks, and solos so you can jam along with your favorite bands. They contain performance notes and an overview of each artist's or group's style, with note-for-note transcriptions in notes and tab. The CDs feature full-band demos at both normal and slow speeds.

AC/DC
14041352.....................................$22.99

ACOUSTIC CLASSICS
00695864.....................................$19.95

AEROSMITH 1973-1979
00695106.....................................$22.95

AEROSMITH 1979-1998
00695219.....................................$22.95

DUANE ALLMAN
00696042.....................................$22.99

BEST OF CHET ATKINS
00695752.....................................$22.95

AVENGED SEVENFOLD
00696473.....................................$22.99

BEST OF THE BEATLES FOR ACOUSTIC GUITAR
00695453.....................................$22.95

THE BEATLES BASS
00695283.....................................$22.95

THE BEATLES FAVORITES
00695096.....................................$24.95

THE BEATLES HITS
00695049.....................................$24.95

JEFF BECK
00696427.....................................$22.99

BEST OF GEORGE BENSON
00695418.....................................$22.95

BEST OF BLACK SABBATH
00695249.....................................$22.95

BLUES BREAKERS WITH JOHN MAYALL & ERIC CLAPTON
00696374.....................................$22.99

BLUES/ROCK GUITAR HEROES
00696381.....................................$19.99

BON JOVI
00696380.....................................$22.99

ROY BUCHANAN
00696654.....................................$22.99

KENNY BURRELL
00695830.....................................$22.99

BEST OF CHARLIE CHRISTIAN
00695584.....................................$22.95

BEST OF ERIC CLAPTON
00695038.....................................$24.95

ERIC CLAPTON – FROM THE ALBUM UNPLUGGED
00695250.....................................$24.95

BEST OF CREAM
00695251.....................................$22.95

CREEDANCE CLEARWATER REVIVAL
00695924.....................................$22.95

DEEP PURPLE – GREATEST HITS
00695625.....................................$22.95

THE BEST OF DEF LEPPARD
00696516.....................................$22.95

TOMMY EMMANUEL
00696409.....................................$22.99

ESSENTIAL JAZZ GUITAR
00695875.....................................$19.99

FAMOUS ROCK GUITAR SOLOS
00695590.....................................$19.95

FLEETWOOD MAC
00696416.....................................$22.99

BEST OF FOO FIGHTERS
00695481.....................................$24.95

ROBBEN FORD
00695903.....................................$22.95

BEST OF GRANT GREEN
00695747.....................................$22.95

BEST OF GUNS N' ROSES
00695183.....................................$24.95

THE BEST OF BUDDY GUY
00695186.....................................$22.99

JIM HALL
00695848.....................................$22.99

JIMI HENDRIX
00696560.....................................$24.95

JIMI HENDRIX – VOLUME 2
00695835.....................................$24.95

JOHN LEE HOOKER
00695894.....................................$19.99

HOT COUNTRY GUITAR
00695580.....................................$19.95

BEST OF JAZZ GUITAR
00695586.....................................$24.95

ERIC JOHNSON
00699317.....................................$24.95

ROBERT JOHNSON
00695264.....................................$22.95

BARNEY KESSEL
00696009.....................................$22.99

THE ESSENTIAL ALBERT KING
00695713.....................................$22.95

B.B. KING – BLUES LEGEND
00696039.....................................$22.99

B.B. KING – THE DEFINITIVE COLLECTION
00695635.....................................$22.95

B.B. KING – MASTER BLUESMAN
00699923.....................................$24.99

BEST OF KISS
00699413.....................................$22.95

MARK KNOPFLER
00695178.....................................$22.95

LYNYRD SKYNYRD
00695872.....................................$24.95

THE BEST OF YNGWIE MALMSTEEN
00695669.....................................$22.95

BEST OF PAT MARTINO
00695632.....................................$24.99

MEGADETH
00696421.....................................$22.99

WES MONTGOMERY
00695387.....................................$24.95

BEST OF NIRVANA
00695483.....................................$24.95

VERY BEST OF OZZY OSBOURNE
00695431.....................................$22.95

BRAD PAISLEY
00696379.....................................$22.99

BEST OF JOE PASS
00695730.....................................$22.95

JACO PASTORIUS
00695544.....................................$24.95

TOM PETTY
00696021.....................................$22.99

PINK FLOYD – EARLY CLASSICS
00695566.....................................$22.95

THE GUITARS OF ELVIS
00696507.....................................$22.95

BEST OF QUEEN
00695097.....................................$24.95

RADIOHEAD
00109304.....................................$24.99

BEST OF RAGE AGAINST THE MACHINE
00695480.....................................$24.95

RED HOT CHILI PEPPERS
00695173.....................................$22.95

RED HOT CHILI PEPPERS – GREATEST HITS
00695828.....................................$24.95

BEST OF DJANGO REINHARDT
00695660.....................................$24.95

BEST OF ROCK 'N' ROLL GUITAR
00695559.....................................$19.95

BEST OF ROCKABILLY GUITAR
00695785.....................................$19.95

THE ROLLING STONES
00695079.....................................$24.95

BEST OF JOE SATRIANI
00695216.....................................$22.95

THE BEST OF SOUL GUITAR
00695703.....................................$19.95

BEST OF SOUTHERN ROCK
00695560.....................................$19.95

STEELY DAN
00696015.....................................$22.99

MIKE STERN
00695800.....................................$24.99

BEST OF SURF GUITAR
00695822.....................................$19.95

BEST OF SYSTEM OF A DOWN
00695788.....................................$22.95

STEVE VAI
00673247.....................................$22.95

STEVE VAI – ALIEN LOVE SECRETS: THE NAKED VAMPS
00695223.....................................$22.95

STEVE VAI – FIRE GARDEN: THE NAKED VAMPS
00695166.....................................$22.95

STEVE VAI – THE ULTRA ZONE: NAKED VAMPS
00695684.....................................$22.95

STEVIE RAY VAUGHAN – 2ND ED.
00699316.....................................$24.95

THE GUITAR STYLE OF STEVIE RAY VAUGHAN
00695155.....................................$24.95

BEST OF THE VENTURES
00695772.....................................$19.95

THE WHO – 2ND ED.
00695561.....................................$22.95

JOHNNY WINTER
00695951.....................................$22.99

YES
00113120.....................................$22.99

NEIL YOUNG – GREATEST HITS
00695988.....................................$22.99

BEST OF ZZ TOP
00695738.....................................$24.95

HAL•LEONARD® CORPORATION
7777 W. BLUEMOUND RD. P.O. BOX 13819
MILWAUKEE, WISCONSIN 53213

www.halleonard.com

COMPLETE DESCRIPTIONS AND SONGLISTS ONLINE!
Prices, contents and availability subject to change without notice.

0215